The Cuban Missile Crisis

The Cuban Missile Crisis

A Concise History

Don Munton
University of Northern British Columbia

David A. Welch
University of Toronto

New York   Oxford
OXFORD UNIVERSITY PRESS
2007

Oxford University Press, Inc., publishes works that further Oxford University's objective of excellence in research, scholarship, and education.

Oxford   New York
Auckland   Cape Town   Dar es Salaam   Hong Kong   Karachi
Kuala Lumpur   Madrid   Melbourne   Mexico City   Nairobi
New Delhi   Shanghai   Taipei   Toronto

With offices in
Argentina   Austria   Brazil   Chile   Czech Republic   France   Greece
Guatemala   Hungary   Italy   Japan   Poland   Portugal   Singapore
South Korea   Switzerland   Thailand   Turkey   Ukraine   Vietnam

Published by Oxford University Press, Inc.
198 Madison Avenue, New York, New York 10016
http://www.oup.com

Oxford is a registered trademark of Oxford University Press

Library of Congress Cataloging-in-Publication Data

Munton, Don.
   The Cuban Missile Crisis: A concise history / Don Munton and David A. Welch.
      p. cm.
   Includes bibliographical references and index.
   ISBN-13: 978-0-19-517859-3—ISBN-13: 978-0-19-517860-9 (pbk.)
   ISBN-10: 0-19-517859-9—ISBN-10: 0-19-517860-2 (pbk.)
   1. Cuban Missile Crisis, 1962.   I. Title: Concise history of the Cuban Missile Crisis.   II. Welch, David A.   III. Title.

E841.M796 2006
973.922—dc22

                                                                  2006040037

Printing number: 9 8 7 6 5 4 3 2 1
Printed in the United States of America
on acid-free paper

For Nathaniel and Sarah

Contents

Acknowledgments

We would like to offer thanks to the many individuals and institutions who made this book possible: for research assistance, Geoffrey Castle, Max Dionisio, Jillian Merrick, Sarah Munton, and David Vogt; for materials, Maryrose Grossman at the John F. Kennedy Library; for comments and suggestions, Robert Beck, James Blight, Robert Cohen, Peter Feaver, Mark Kramer, janet Lang, Mitchell Lerner, Jennifer See, and one anonymous reviewer; and for financial support, the Social Sciences and Humanities Research Council of Canada, the University of Northern British Columbia, the University of British Columbia, and the Rockefeller Foundation's Bellagio Study and Conference Center. Special thanks to our acquiring editor, Peter Coveney, who helped shape the book conceptually and who displayed boundless enthusiasm and patience. Any errors, of course, are ours alone.

Don Munton
David A. Welch

List of Acronyms

CIA	Central Intelligence Agency
CINCLANT	Commander in Chief, Atlantic Command
COMOR	Committee on Overhead Reconnaissance
DCI	Director of Central Intelligence
DEFCON	Defense Condition (US alert status)
DGI	*Dirección General de Inteligencia* (Cuban intelligence)
ExComm	Executive Committee of the US National Security Council
FKR	*Frontovaya Krylaya Raketa*, early Soviet cruise missile, deployed to Cuba
GRU	*Glavnoye Razvedyvatelnoye Upravlenie*, Soviet military intelligence agency
HUMINT	Human intelligence
ICBM	Intercontinental ballistic missile
INF	Intermediate-range nuclear forces
IRBM	Intermediate-range ballistic missile
JCS	Joint Chiefs of Staff
KGB	*Komitet Gosudarstvennoĭ Bezopasnosti*, Soviet intelligence and security agency
LTBT	Limited Test Ban Treaty (also sometimes called PTBT, see below)
MRBM	Medium-range ballistic missile
NATO	North Atlantic Treaty Organization
NPIC	National Photographic Interpretation Center
NSAM	National Security Action Memorandum
OAS	Organization of American States
OPLAN	Operational plan
PHOTINT	Photo intelligence
POL	Petroleum, oil, and lubricants
PSP	*Partido Socialista Popular* (Cuban Communist Party)
PTBT	Partial Test Ban Treaty (also sometimes called LTBT, see above)

SAC	Strategic Air Command, US Air Force
SACEUR	NATO Supreme Allied Commander, Europe
SAM	Surface to air missile
SGA	Special Group (Augmented)
SIGINT	Signals intelligence
SLBM	Submarine-launched ballistic missile
SNIE	Special National Intelligence Estimate
TSD	Technical Services Division, CIA
UN	United Nations
USAF	US Air Force
USIA	US Information Agency
USSR	Union of Soviet Socialist Republics

Dramatis Personae

(and Positions in October 1962)

Acheson, Dean	Former US secretary of state
Adenauer, Konrad	Chancellor of West Germany
Alekseev, Aleksandr I.	Soviet ambassador to Cuba
Alsop, Stewart	Journalist
Anderson, Adm. George	Chief of naval operations
Anderson, Maj. Rudolf	U-2 pilot (USAF), shot down over Cuba, October 27, 1962
Aragonés Navarro, Emilio	Member, Secretariat and Political Bureau, Cuba
Ball, George W.	Undersecretary of state
Bartlett, Charles	Journalist and Kennedy family friend
Batista, Fulgencio	Former Cuban dictator, overthrown by Castro
Biryuzov, Marshal S. S.	Commander-in-chief of the Strategic Rocket Forces, USSR
Bohlen, Charles E.	Former US ambassador to the USSR and newly appointed US ambassador to France
Bolshakov, Georgi N.	Soviet intelligence officer (GRU), Washington
Brandt, Willy	Mayor of West Berlin
Brezhnev, Leonid I.	President of the Presidium of the Supreme Soviet
Bundy, McGeorge	Special assistant to the president for national security affairs
Capehart, Homer	Senator (R-IN)
Carter, Lt. Gen. Marshall	Deputy director of the CIA
Castro, Fidel	Prime minister of Cuba
Castro, Raúl	Minister of the Armed Forces and vice premier, Cuba
de Gaulle, Charles	President of France

Dennison, Adm. Robert	CINCLANT
Diefenbaker, John	Prime minister of Canada
Dillon, C. Douglas	Secretary of the Treasury
Dobrynin, Anatoly	Soviet ambassador to the United States
Eisenhower, Dwight D.	Former president of the United States
Fanfani, Amintore	President of Italy
Feklisov, Aleksandr	KGB station chief, Soviet embassy in Washington (alias Alexander Fomin)
Fomin, Alexander	*See* Feklisov, Aleksandr
Goldwater, Barry	Senator (R-AZ)
Gribkov, Gen. Anatoly I.	Deputy head of the General Staff Main Operations Directorate, USSR
Gromyko, Andrei	Foreign minister, USSR
Guevara, Ernesto ("Che")	Minister of industry, Cuba, and close friend of Fidel Castro
Heyser, Maj. Richard S.	U-2 pilot (USAF)
Holeman, Frank	Journalist
Ivanov, Col. Gen. Semyon P.	Secretary to the Defense Council and head of the General Staff Main Operations Directorate, USSR
Johnson, Lyndon B.	Vice president of the United States
Johnson, U. Alexis	Deputy undersecretary of state for political affairs
Keating, Kenneth	Senator (R-NY)
Kennedy, John F.	President of the United States
Kennedy, Robert F. (Bobby)	Attorney general of the United States
Khrushchev, Nikita S.	First secretary, Central Committee of the Communist Party of the Soviet Union, and Soviet premier
Knox, William	President, Westinghouse International
Lansdale, Brig. Gen. Edward G.	Head of Operation Mongoose
Lechuga, Carlos	Cuban ambassador to the UN
Lundahl, Arthur C.	Director, National Photographic Interpretation Center
Macmillan, Harold	Prime minister of the United Kingdom
Malinovsky, Rodion Ya.	Minister of defense, USSR
Martin, Edwin M.	Assistant secretary of state for inter-American affairs
McCone, John J.	Director of central intelligence
McNamara, Robert S.	Secretary of defense, United States
Mikoyan, Anastas	First deputy premier, USSR
Mikoyan, Sergo	Son of Anastas Mikoyan
Mundt, Karl	Senator (R-SD)
Nehru, Jawaharlal	Prime minister of India

Nixon, Richard	Gubernatorial candidate in California, former vice president of the United States
Norstad, Gen. Lauris	SACEUR
Ormsby-Gore, David	British ambassador to the United States and Kennedy family friend
Penkovsky, Lt. Col. Oleg	Officer, GRU, and Western spy
Pliyev, Gen. Issa A.	Commander-in-chief, Soviet Group of Forces, Cuba
Powers, Francis Gary	U-2 pilot (CIA) shot down over Soviet Union, May 1, 1960
Roa, Raúl	Foreign minister of Cuba
Rusk, Dean	Secretary of state
Salinger, Pierre	White House press secretary
Scali, John	Journalist
Schlesinger, Arthur M., Jr.	Special assistant to the president, White House
Shoup, Gen. David M.	Commandant of the US Marine Corps
Sorensen, Theodore C.	Special counsel to the president
Stevenson, Adlai	US ambassador to the UN
Sweeney, Gen. Walter C.	Commander, Tactical Air Command, USAF
Taylor, Gen. Maxwell D.	Chairman, Joint Chiefs of Staff (after October 1, 1962)
Thant, U	Acting secretary general of the UN
Thompson, Llewellyn E.	Former ambassador to the USSR
Tower, John	Senator (R-TX)
Voronkov, Col. Georgy	Commander, Soviet SAM site, Banes
Zorin, Valerian	Soviet ambassador to the UN

The Cuban Missile Crisis

Introduction: The REAL Thirteen Days?

The Cuban missile crisis was the most dangerous event in human history.

In October 1962, the world held its breath to see whether the United States and the USSR would come to nuclear blows over Soviet Chairman Nikita Khrushchev's attempt to deploy nuclear weapons to Cuba. US President John F. Kennedy had warned that he would not tolerate "offensive" Soviet weapons in America's backyard, but Khrushchev had already authorized a secret deployment of precisely the kind that Kennedy feared. When US intelligence discovered missile sites under construction in Cuba, Kennedy demanded that Khrushchev dismantle them and imposed a naval "quarantine" to signal his resolve. Khrushchev railed against Kennedy's "illegal" blockade and initially refused to back down. Cuba and the USSR were both sovereign countries, Khrushchev insisted, that had every right to conclude military agreements as they saw fit. Besides, the United States had deployed similar missiles right next door to the Soviet Union in Turkey.

For several days, the superpowers stood eyeball to eyeball. The tension mounted. War seemed more and more likely. Hope for a peaceful settlement seemed to slip away. But these were days of somber reflection for Kennedy and Khrushchev, and as the clock ticked, both had a gradual change of heart. They became acutely aware of the danger that the crisis could spin out of control. They were very worried that accidents, misperceptions, and unintended actions could trigger unwanted escalation. If the situation got completely out of hand, the superpowers could find themselves fighting a third world war. In the first two world wars, millions of people had died, but the carnage took years. This time, literally *hundreds* of millions could die in a matter of hours or days.

At the eleventh hour, Kennedy and Khrushchev struck a deal. Khrushchev publicly agreed to withdraw the weapons Kennedy considered offensive, and Kennedy publicly pledged not to invade Cuba, once international inspectors had confirmed the Soviet withdrawal. There was a crucial side agreement as well: Kennedy promised to remove American missiles from

Turkey "within a few months"—though this part of the deal would remain secret for more than twenty years.

Because the Cuban missile crisis was such a dangerous event, it has been closely studied. Library shelves groan under the weight of lengthy books examining it from every possible angle. But most people know about it from one of two sources—both titled, ironically, "thirteen days," in reference to the length of the period between the American discovery of the Soviet deployment on October 15, 1962, and Khrushchev's agreement to withdraw the missiles on October 28.

The first of these is a short book, *Thirteen Days: A Memoir of the Cuban Missile Crisis*, by Robert F. Kennedy (aka "R. F. K." or "Bobby"), the president's brother and attorney general. President Kennedy's former special assistant for national security affairs, McGeorge Bundy, used to tell a story about Bobby Kennedy's *Thirteen Days*. When R. F. K. completed the manuscript in 1968, the year he entered the Democratic presidential primaries, he circulated it among close friends and associates for their comments and suggestions. According to Bundy, R. F. K. gave a copy to Kenneth O'Donnell, part of the president's "Irish mafia" of political advisers and fixers, and then called him up several days later to ask him what he thought of it. "It's very interesting, Bobby," O'Donnell reportedly said. "But I thought your brother had something to do with solving the Cuban missile crisis." "Well, he did," Bobby replied. "But he isn't running for president this year."

That very same O'Donnell is the character played by Kevin Costner in the film *Thirteen Days*, the other well-known source. In the film, it is O'Donnell who manages to save the world from nuclear war by bucking up the president's courage, talking him down from his bouts of anger and melancholy, fixing him drinks at crucial moments, and acting as his secret direct back channel to pilots of reconnaissance planes. The film makes for gripping viewing, but one might easily imagine R. F. K. watching it today and saying to Costner, "Gosh, Kevin, I thought my brother had something to do with solving the Cuban missile crisis."

Both of these *Thirteen Days* have great merit in particular respects. They succeed brilliantly, for example, in conveying the tension and high drama of the crisis. But as histories, they are profoundly flawed. First, they both present an account of the event as seen entirely through American eyes. Soviets and Cubans are essentially absent. Neither tells us anything about why Khrushchev tried to sneak missiles into Cuba, why Fidel Castro played along, why they thought they could get away with it, or what transpired in Moscow or Havana that permitted the superpowers to step gingerly back from the nuclear brink. Second, they concentrate overwhelmingly on a particular two-week period, providing no context to help us understand what led to those climactic events, nor what happened afterward as a result of them. Third, neither takes full advantage of the revolution in missile crisis scholarship made possible first by Soviet President Mikhail Gorbachev and his policy of *glasnost'* ("openness"), by the collapse of the Soviet Union, by Cuban participation in oral histories of the event, and by the truly massive declassification of once-secret documents, both in the United States and elsewhere. Kennedy's *Thirteen Days* could not have benefited from any of this, of course, because it predated them all. Costner's makes a sincere effort to do so but one limited inevitably and understandably by time constraints and the requirements of theatricality (the movie is, after all, first and foremost entertainment). Both, in short, are full of errors.

Our aim in this book is to provide a narrative and interpretation of this most dangerous event that is at once concise, accurate, and up-to-date. To do this effectively, we believe, it is vital to resist the common temptation to focus exclusively on the two-week period in October 1962 that represented the moment of maximum danger. The Cuban missile crisis was the product of deep historical forces and of clashing worldviews, and to understand it properly, one must spend some time putting it into context. It also had profound consequences not just for the leaders of the countries who stood on the nuclear brink, and for their citizens, but for the entire world. The Cuban missile crisis continues to reverberate today. It is difficult to overstate its historical importance.

Since we seek to provide a "big picture" view of the crisis, our attempt to be concise means that we cannot try to be exhaustive. Our goal here is to throw into relatively sharp relief the underlying dynamics, the principal events, and the most significant consequences of the event. Fortunately, there are bookshelves full of very long and detailed histories, many of which are excellent; and for readers who are searching for more focused and more finely grained treatments, we provide a bibliographic essay at the end for guidance.

We are acutely aware of two limitations that commonly frustrate any attempt to be both accurate and up-to-date. The first of these is the simple fact that to make sense of events one must interpret them, and interpretation is always subject to dispute. The second is the even simpler fact that to make sense of events one must be able to know exactly what those events were. The Cuban missile crisis—certainly one of the most studied and most thoroughly documented historical events of all time—nicely illustrates both of these limitations. Historians continue to disagree about its proper interpretation. New information continues to surface all the time. The history of the Cuban missile crisis, in other words, is both inherently controversial and something of a moving target. We set out to write the *REAL Thirteen Days*, and we tell the tale to the best of our ability in the space available, but we are under no illusion that ours, or anyone else's, can truly be definitive. Since we believe the controversies and uncertainties are instructive in their own right, we have chosen to highlight at various places precisely the key issues that generate debate or about which there remains considerable doubt. Nevertheless, decades of missile crisis scholarship have succeeded in pushing back the frontiers of uncertainty. We can have much higher confidence today in the tale that we tell than first- or second-generation historians had in theirs, quite simply because there is so much more material now available on which to draw. Since a number of early histories continue to be popular and widely read, we have chosen to highlight some of the crucial respects in which the story of the crisis has changed over the years by means of brief sidebars bringing them to the fore.

We begin in Chapter 1 with background, situating the Cuban missile crisis in the immediate context of the Cold War but also in the deeper context of US–Cuban relations, which had a profound effect on the trajectory the Cuban Revolution took under Fidel Castro. In this chapter, we develop two themes that we believe are crucially important for understanding how the world's two superpowers could stumble into a nuclear crisis with essentially no warning whatsoever. The first theme is that policymakers in all three countries—the United States, the Soviet Union, and Cuba—acted on the basis of perceptions and judgments deeply informed by their own historical perspectives and experiences, largely oblivious to the fact that their counterparts' perspectives and experiences were radically different in important respects. By freely indulging in *mirror-imaging,* or assuming that others saw the world the same way they did, all three miscalculated the consequences of their own actions and failed to anticipate the actions of the others. Put another way, empathy was in short supply in 1962.[1] The second theme is that policymakers in all three countries acted on the basis of beliefs that they did not subject to careful critical scrutiny. Stereotypes, aphorisms, maxims, and deductions from first principles guided policy choices that should have been guided instead by openness to information that challenged prior beliefs. Taken together, these two related themes suggest that with a little more empathy and circumspection, Kennedy, Khrushchev, and Castro might not have led the world to the brink of nuclear war. The Cuban missile crisis, in other words, was a mistake, one for which leaders in all three countries must share the blame. This, of course, contrasts with the traditional interpretation of the Cuban missile crisis in the American literature as a nefarious Soviet challenge that simply blindsided an innocent United States.

In Chapter 2, we discuss the events of what we might call the "long summer" of 1962 (April through October), which was the prelude to the crisis. Here, we examine the details of the Soviet missile deployment to Cuba, the game of cat-and-mouse between the three countries' intelligence

---

1. As we are using the term here, *empathy* refers to the capacity to understand how another feels and sees the world. This is distinct from *sympathy,* which is the capacity actually to feel what another feels or to share another's view of the world. Given their many ideological and cultural differences, there was essentially no chance that Kennedy, Khrushchev, and Castro could have sympathized with one another. However, had they made an effort, they could have understood each other better.

communities, and the mounting warnings, signals, and eventual discovery of the Soviet deployment by American photoreconnaissance. Our discussion in this chapter is more strictly descriptive and less thickly interpretive than that in Chapter 1, but the themes we explore in Chapter 1 resurface here as well. Khrushchev underestimated the risks of a premature American discovery of the deployment because of mirror-imaging, wishful thinking, and a willful blindness that had its roots both in self-righteousness and in a sense of desperation that the secret deployment not fail. Kennedy underestimated the risk that Khrushchev would take in trying to deploy nuclear weapons to Cuba because he could not imagine either that Khrushchev could find such a reckless gamble attractive or, if he did, that he could fail to appreciate the difficult position in which his actions would put Kennedy. Ironically, it was Castro who saw the looming crisis earliest and made an effort, timid and unsuccessful though it was, to forestall it.

In Chapter 3, we look at American decision making between the discovery of the missiles on October 15, 1962, and President Kennedy's choice of a naval "quarantine" in response. In this week of agonizing deliberation, President Kennedy and his closest advisers confronted for the first time the knowledge that the premises of their own policy had been deeply flawed. They realized that they had profoundly misunderstood Khrushchev and that Khrushchev had profoundly misunderstood them. This dawning realization had a very salutary effect: after an initial wave of anger and belligerence, Kennedy began to ask hard questions about his own understanding and to work very hard to cultivate the empathy that had been so absent before. This induced a healthy caution and a healthy concern not to take steps that would leave his adversaries no peaceful way out. Several days' opportunity to deliberate in private proved crucial for a successful, peaceful resolution of the crisis. One wonders what would have happened if Kennedy had not had that opportunity, as he almost certainly would not have had today. The press, although it caught wind of the looming crisis before Kennedy had finally decided how to handle it, deferred to his request not to print the story. It is difficult to imagine today's press corps being quite so accommodating. Kennedy would have had far less time to think through his options.

Chapter 4 deals with the public week of the crisis, from Kennedy's speech to the nation on October 22, announcing the discovery of the Soviet deployment and his choice of a quarantine in response, to the dramatic climax and breakthrough on the weekend of October 27–28. These six days were the Cuban missile crisis as most of the world experienced it—the anguished days of fear and uncertainty, when it seemed that World War III might break out at any moment. This was a period of frenzied activity in Washington, Moscow, and Havana as all three leaders did their best to steer events in a particular direction. During this time, Kennedy single-mindedly sought a peaceful resolution of the crisis that would satisfy his minimum demand that Khrushchev withdraw "offensive" weapons from Cuba. Khrushchev, in contrast, began the week experiencing the very shock, anger, and belligerence that Kennedy had experienced upon discovering the deployment but very quickly underwent the same transformation to circumspection and caution that Kennedy had undergone the week before. Castro, convinced that Cuba was on the verge of its decisive historical showdown with the United States, spent most of the week trying to prevent Khrushchev's will from weakening and doing his best, unwittingly or not, to provoke the very confrontation that Kennedy and Khrushchev were trying to avoid. Castro's efforts to buck up Khrushchev's courage backfired: they merely convinced him to settle all the more quickly. Both Kennedy and Khrushchev were gradually coming to appreciate the importance of settling in any case because as they groped their way toward a solution, they could see that events were beginning to spin out of control. What they knew was frightening enough; what they did not know would have frightened them even more.

Chapter 5 covers the aftermath of the crisis, from Castro's furious reaction to the news that Khrushchev had agreed to settle to Khrushchev's efforts to calm him down and enlist his cooperation, and from the initial failure of American and Soviet negotiators to agree on exactly what Khrushchev had committed to withdraw from Cuba (which almost caused the deal to fall apart) to the final settlement and its lingering ambiguities. Here, we also discuss the steps Kennedy and Khrushchev took to try to make future such crises less likely and the longer-term legacy of the crisis, which had both positive and negative elements, the latter of which had a great deal to do with the fact that neither Kennedy nor Khrushchev remained in office long afterward. Their respective successors had less nuanced understandings of the lessons of the crisis and failed to capitalize upon the opportunities the missile crisis presented to deepen US–Soviet understanding and tone down US–Cuban hostility. We return in the conclusion to our overarching themes and to the question of what we can learn about world politics, and indeed about history, from this pivotal event.

Finally, we provide at the end a bibliographic essay designed in part to assist further reading and in part to indicate some of the most important sources of information and insight upon which we have drawn. Again, this essay is not exhaustive, but we believe it provides a good short catalogue of the best available material. Much of it confirms our interpretations, but of course much of it also challenges them. At the end of the day, readers will have to decide for themselves whether there is, in fact, a "real" thirteen days after all.

CHAPTER 1

Background to the Crisis

WE RIGHTLY THINK of the Cuban missile crisis as a Cold War crisis. It took place almost in the middle of a nearly fifty-year period of intense hostility and rivalry between the world's two superpowers, the United States and the Soviet Union, and their respective alliance systems, the North Atlantic Treaty Organization (NATO, led by the United States) and the Warsaw Treaty Organization (more commonly known as the Warsaw Pact, led by the Union of Soviet Socialist Republics [USSR]). The *Cold War* is a particularly good term for the period between World War II and the collapse of the Soviet Union—from the late 1940s to 1990—because, despite the intense hostility between these two camps, they never actually fought a "hot" war. The Cuban missile crisis is the closest they came.

The United States and the Soviet Union not only were the two most powerful countries in the world during this period but they also championed very different values and visions. The United States stood for liberal democracy and market capitalism. The Soviet Union stood for socialism and a command economy. Each managed to construe the other as inevitably hostile and, indeed, evil. Each managed to understand itself as standing on the right side of history and on the defensive against the predatory instincts, needs, and desires of the other. This meant that conflicts of interest between so-called East and West—the socialist bloc and the "free world"—took on the character of a moral struggle. Neither side had much interest in, or hope for, dialogue and compromise. Both relied upon threats—principally military threats—to keep the other at bay. Hence, the Cold War was a time of intense rivalry, constant high levels of alert, and, most frighteningly, extremely high levels of nuclear armament. In short, for most of the Cold War, the world stood perilously close to the nuclear brink. The only relief came in occasional periods during which tensions seemed to ease and the danger of hot war seemed to recede somewhat. These periods generally came to be known by the French word *détente*.

The United States and the Soviet Union were both extremely powerful, but there were significant differences between them. Throughout the Cold War, the United States was by far the richer country. It also acquired nuclear weapons earlier and, until the 1970s, enjoyed considerable superiority in nuclear capability, in terms of both the quantity and quality of its weapons. But the Soviet Union had by far the larger army and seemed capable of overwhelming NATO forces in Europe relatively quickly should a hot war begin in earnest. Thus, NATO relied upon the threat of nuclear retaliation to keep the Soviet Union in check. Once the Soviet Union acquired a significant nuclear capability of its own in the 1960s (exactly when is a matter of debate), the two countries found themselves in a condition of "mutual assured destruction," known by its strangely appropriate acronym MAD. Each used the threat of annihilating the other to deter reckless adventurism.

The United States and Joseph Stalin's Soviet Union had been allies against Nazi Germany in World War II, but with the defeat of their common enemy in 1945, the stark contradictions between liberal democracy and Soviet-style socialism came to the fore. Of particular importance at this time was the fact that the superpowers were unable to agree on the long-term status of Germany in general or of its capital, Berlin. Each was divided into four zones of occupation: American, British, French, and Soviet. The Soviet zone of occupation in East Germany surrounded the city of Berlin proper, effectively cutting off the Western powers' access to their occupation zones. A provisional agreement called for temporary access routes across East German territory and air corridors through which the Western allies would be permitted to fly personnel and supplies. But the Western understanding was that the Soviet Union would ultimately withdraw from its occupied territories in Eastern Europe, giving the inhabitants of eastern Germany, Poland, Hungary, Czechoslovakia, and the Baltic states a chance to determine their own fates democratically. To some extent, Stalin simply could not resist the opportunity to maintain the influence of the Soviet Union in this area. But the USSR was also eager never to suffer invasion from the West again, as had Russia in 1812 and 1941, and, to that end, Stalin felt justified in establishing a buffer zone of friendly states and forcibly deindustrializing the part of Germany that he controlled. When Soviet forces failed to withdraw from Eastern Europe and when the Soviet Union made clear that it had no intention of demobilizing to the extent that the United States and Britain had done, it seemed as though an "Iron Curtain" had descended across Europe, as British Prime Minister Winston Churchill put it in a famous speech at Westminster College in Fulton, Missouri, on March 5, 1946.

The Cold War had several implications for Latin America in general, and for Cuba in particular. As the United States devoted resources and attention to rebuilding Western Europe, it was in effect creating competition for Latin American industry, inflating the costs of Latin American imports, and generating Latin American resentment. The United States came to perceive Latin American problems increasingly in Cold War terms when Latin American leaders themselves largely saw them in simple economic and social justice terms.

As part of its effort to buttress the Western Hemisphere against Soviet encroachment and to cultivate Latin American sympathies, the United States helped create the Organization of American States (OAS) in 1951. Article 15 of the OAS charter enshrined the principle of non-intervention, much to the delight of Latin American states. Yet, just three years later, the Central Intelligence Agency (CIA) brought down the duly elected Guatemalan government of Jacobo Arbenz Guzmán simply because he sought land reform, thereby threatening the holdings of powerful American agricultural interests. Any Latin American leader interested in land reform, the US government believed, must have communist sympathies.

It is important to note that American and Soviet leaders both saw the Cuban missile crisis against this background. From the American perspective, it was first and foremost a Soviet challenge in an American sphere of vital interest. As such, it had to be resisted, according to the dictates of power politics and the standard Cold War logic of the day. If the Soviet deployment of nuclear missiles in the Western Hemisphere had gone unchallenged, American leaders believed, Soviet leaders would be convinced that the United States lacked the will to resist further challenges and would simply mount more of them elsewhere. Other countries would also doubt American resolve to resist Soviet expansion, and some of them would lean toward Moscow or fall to communist insurgencies. Soviet leaders saw the deployment as a necessary step to protect and secure the allegiance of a fellow socialist state and to shore up Soviet deterrent capabilities, which proved to be far weaker at the time than the Soviets had claimed and that the US administration of President Dwight D. Eisenhower had believed.

Both ways of understanding the problem neglected to consider the vital history of US–Cuban relations. If US–Cuban relations had been different, Fidel Castro might never have come to power—or, if he had, he might have been on friendly terms with Washington. Hostility between Castro and the United States is precisely what provided the Soviet Union with the opportunity to try to protect a friendly socialist state in the Western Hemisphere and to take advantage of Cuba's geographical position to shore up its nuclear inferiority. Without this hostility, in short, there would have been no Soviet challenge for the United States to resist. Castro therefore played a crucial role in the genesis of the Cuban missile crisis. The fact that *he* saw the crisis primarily in a historical US–Cuban relations frame, rather than a Cold War frame, is an important fact generally overlooked, not merely by US policymakers at the time but also by scholars ever since.

US–Cuban Relations in Historical Perspective

It was a common view in the early American republic that Cuba, then a Spanish colony, would eventually become part of the United States. As Secretary of

State John Quincy Adams said in 1823, Cuba was "an object of transcendent importance to the political and commercial interests of our Union":

> Its commanding position, with reference to the Gulf of Mexico, and the West India seas; the character of its population; its situation midway between our Southern Coast, and the Island of St. Domingo; its safe and capacious harbor of Havanna [sic] fronting a long line of our shores destitute of the same advantage; the nature of its productions, and of its wants furnishing the supplies and needing the returns of a commerce immensely profitable, and mutually beneficial, give it an importance in the sum of our national interests with which that of no other foreign Territory can be compared, and little inferior to that which binds the different members of this Union together.

Adams believed that the "laws of political gravitation" would draw Cuba to the United States, and many Americans were eager to see Cuba's destiny fulfilled. One such person was President James K. Polk, who in 1848 went so far as to offer to buy it.

Slavery frustrated American annexationist designs prior to the Civil War. It was impossible to bring Cuba into the Union without disrupting the delicate balance in the Senate between free states and slave states. Cuba had more slaves per capita than anywhere in the world. Some thought that simultaneously annexing Canada and Cuba would solve this particular problem since slavery was illegal in Canada. But few Canadians looked with favor on the idea, and forcing the matter would require taking on Canada's colonial masters, the British, who were at the peak of their global power in the nineteenth century. Cuba's Spanish colonial masters were bungling their rule and alienating increasingly large numbers of Cubans, but disaffected Cubans preferred independence to union with the United States. Many Americans supported Cuban independence, being philosophically predisposed toward decolonization; but many, including many American leaders, worried rather paternalistically that Cuba was not ready for it. Still others worried that an independent Cuba would quickly fall into British or French hands, giving one of these great naval powers a strategic stranglehold on the Caribbean and potentially control of a future canal across Central America. For these reasons, American leaders were unwilling simply to let the chips in Cuba fall where they may.

The Civil War and Reconstruction temporarily pushed Cuba off the American political agenda, but increasingly bold action on the part of Cuban insurgents and increasingly repressive responses on the part of the Spanish brought matters to a head at the end of the nineteenth century. The most infamous response to Cuban insurrection was the policy of "reconcentration," implemented in February 1896 by the newly appointed Spanish captain general, Valeriano Weyler. Under this policy, Spanish authorities herded entire populations of districts into camps surrounded by trenches and barbed wire, proclaiming anyone found outside fair game to be shot on sight. The camps were far too small to handle the numbers they contained, and hundreds of thousands died of starvation and disease, triggering an outburst of humanitarian outrage in the United States that was gleefully fanned by the "yellow press," led by William Randolph Hearst's *New York Journal* and Joseph Pulitzer's *New York World*, then engaged in a bitter circulation war. In addition to being an obvious humanitarian disaster, the civil strife in Cuba was costing the United States a fortune in lost trade and investment.

President William McKinley issued an ultimatum to the Spanish government in 1897, demanding it cease its repression in Cuba. The Spanish complied to some extent, but the Cuban insurgents, sensing the tide turning in their favor, kept up the pressure and the conflict escalated. Concerned about the prospect of anarchy on the island, McKinley sought to signal American concern by dispatching the armored cruiser *Maine* to Havana Harbor, where it mysteriously exploded and sank with heavy loss of life on February 15, 1898. There is no proof that Spain was responsible, and it is difficult to imagine what Spain could possibly have gained by sabotaging an American warship; however, an outraged American public blamed Spain anyway. McKinley asked Congress for permission to intervene; Spain severed diplomatic relations in protest; and Congress, not to be outdone by Spain, retroactively declared war.

The Spanish–American War was quick and one-sided. By the middle of the summer, the United States found itself in control of most of the Spanish empire, including Cuba, Puerto Rico, and the Philippines. Although Congress had authorized American military intervention, it had done so explicitly disavowing any intention to control Cuba. A congressional resolution adopted without dissent stated "That the United States hereby disclaims any disposition or intention to exercise sovereignty, jurisdiction, or control over the said island except for the pacification thereof, and asserts its determination, when that is accomplished, to leave the government and control of the island to its people." Nevertheless, the United States ruled Cuba, directly and indirectly, for sixty years.

Cuban resentment at what many perceived as the United States' opportunistic intervention in 1898 lingers to this day, in part because the Castro regime has cultivated it to legitimize its rule and to shift blame for Cuba's economic woes and repressive politics. Cuban schoolchildren are taught that Cubans fought and died for their independence from Spain only to have the United States snatch the prize from their grasp and impose its own version of colonial rule.

American forces occupied Cuba until 1902 and withdrew only after Cuban leaders agreed to authorize future American intervention by incorporating into the Cuban constitution the Platt amendment, which gave the United States the right to intervene under certain circumstances and required Cuba to lease or sell lands for American coaling stations or naval bases (hence the continued anomalous presence on Cuban soil of an

American base at Guantánamo Bay).[1] This, like the Platt amendment itself, is a powerful symbol of "*Yanqui* imperialism" in Cuba today.

Though nominally independent since 1902, Cuba was, until 1959, little more than an American protectorate. Although President Franklin Delano Roosevelt officially gave up the United States' right of intervention in 1934, the American ambassador in Havana was in many respects a more powerful political figure than the Cuban president himself. Cuban leaders rarely made important decisions without consulting Washington, and Americans owned or controlled the most lucrative properties and businesses in Cuba. To Cuban eyes, America genuinely did look like a colonial master. But few Americans saw things this way. Most—including most American presidents—understood American policy toward Cuba as at least benign and perhaps even noble, a view captured well by the prominent historian Samuel Flagg Bemis, who wrote in 1943, "If ever there were an emblem of pride on the escutcheon of American idealism, it is the attitude in our century of the Continental Republic toward Cuba. The urge to annex was there, no doubt, for a century, but it was bridled, curbed, and halted by a great and historic self-denial, checked by the common people of the United States and their opposition to imperialism." Many Americans genuinely felt that they were doing Cuba a favor by liberating it from Spain and keeping it from sliding into anarchy and destitution. This smug, paternalistic attitude kindled profound outrage in Cuba.

No one felt this outrage more acutely than Fidel Castro Ruz, a Jesuit-educated illegitimate son of an illiterate but relatively well-to-do sugar plantation owner and his upstairs maid. Born in 1926, Castro was a lawyer by training but a rebel by disposition. From student activism he moved quickly into political insurrection, gaining notoriety in a quixotic attack on the Moncada Barracks in 1953, a botched effort that landed him in jail for two years but made him a national hero. Released in 1955, Castro and his brother Raúl traveled in Mexico and the United States to drum up support for guerrilla warfare against Cuban dictator Fulgencio Batista. While in Mexico, they met freelance Argentine revolutionary Ernesto "Che" Guevara, who had left Guatemala after the 1954 coup. Together with 79 like-minded adventurers, they landed in Cuba in December 1956 aboard the barely seaworthy yacht *Granmá* with the goal of ousting Batista. The *Granmá* was designed to hold a dozen men comfortably. Grossly overloaded with men, ammunition, and fuel and relentlessly harried by Cuban forces, it somehow managed to land. But only twelve of its occupants—miraculously including both Castro brothers and Che Guevara—eluded death or capture and made their way to the Sierra Maestra to begin organizing a guerrilla war in earnest.

---

1. The Platt amendment was an amendment to the Army Appropriations Bill of March 1901.

From the mountains, Castro conducted hit-and-run operations on Batista's forces. He broadcast defiant radio messages. He gave interviews to foreign journalists, who fawned over him and his dashing band of fellow freedom fighters, dubbed *los barbudos*, or "the bearded ones." Before long the Castro mystique took hold, his forces swelled, and fortune began to smile on his efforts. Batista's army fought half-heartedly, completely incompetently and simply melted away. On January 1, 1959, Batista fled. A week later, Castro rode triumphantly into Havana.

Since the Cuban leaders and elite had benefited handsomely from American patronage, they had been generally happy to support the United States' anticommunist agenda in the hemisphere. And since Fidel Castro's agenda included both reducing American influence in Cuba and promoting

Figure 1.1 Fidel Castro in the Sierra Maestra (Library of Congress)

WAS CASTRO A COMMUNIST?

In many ways, Fidel Castro has always been an enigmatic figure. One matter that has always been a subject of debate is his attachment to communism. Is he, in fact, a communist? If so, for how long has he been one?

There is no easy answer to the first question because much depends upon the definition of terms. There is no doubt that Castro has always been a fierce Cuban nationalist. Theoretically, a true communist cannot be a nationalist: a communist world, in a Marxist sense, would be a world without state borders. But many who have considered themselves communists have embraced nationalism as a vehicle for promoting communist revolution.

There is no doubt also that Castro has always had a strong notion of social justice, in which all members of society have access to basic goods, such as housing, health care, and education. But one does not have to be a communist to hold this view. Social democrats even in capitalist societies do, for example.

The Cuban Communist Party is the only official party in Cuba, and the Cuban state is organized institutionally much like any other communist state. Some argue that this reflects Castro's cynical calculation that it would help secure his rule to embrace communism in this way. By embracing communism, Castro simultaneously managed (a) to enlist the Soviet Union's aid, (b) to co-opt certain communist groups that might eventually have opposed his rule, and (c) to purge certain hard-line communists who were certain to do so.

We will never know for sure whether Castro sincerely embraced communism as an ideology and, if so, when. In large part, this is because Castro is a shrewd political calculator who tells history in different ways depending upon his needs at any given time. He has fairly consistently claimed that he came to communism only after becoming active politically, though he has given different accounts of when, claiming sometimes, for instance, that it happened during his student days and sometimes that it was after the attack on the Moncada Barracks in 1953. Important members of his movement—his brother Raúl and Che Guevara, for instance—clearly came to communism much earlier and were considerably more doctrinaire.

precisely the kinds of economic and political reforms that had provoked American intervention in Guatemala, American leaders quickly began to have doubts about his true colors. Many Americans actually sympathized with Castro in the late 1950s and saw him as a daring, romantic figure struggling to overthrow a corrupt and unpopular dictator. To cultivate American support, Castro went out of his way to keep his distance from communism, even to the point of being openly hostile to the Cuban Communist Party. During the Eisenhower administration, he largely succeeded. Indeed, in 1958 the United States suspended arms shipments to Batista and cultivated ties with

Castro's movement. As long as the Cuban Revolution looked like a home-grown, noncommunist uprising, Washington was content to let it run its course. But some were wary. Vice President Richard Nixon, for example, after meeting Castro in April 1959, decided that he was "either incredibly naive about communism or under Communist discipline."

Whether or not Castro was a true believer in Marxism, as he claimed in November 1960 he had been since his student days, he had to co-opt as much of the communist opposition to Batista as he could and purge the rest in order to consolidate his rule. Some of his associates, such as Osvaldo Dorticós, Aníbal Escalante, and Blas Roca, were members of the *Partido Socialista Popular* (PSP) and devoted followers of Moscow's line. Raúl Castro had long been a member of the PSP as well, and by some accounts he actually kept his membership secret from Fidel for many years, though Raúl's style of revolution, like Che Guevara's, had in many respects more in common with the Maoist than the Soviet model. Fidel needed men like these, but he had to be careful that they did not become rivals. He also needed a great power patron to insulate Cuba from the inevitable American backlash when he took steps to reduce US economic and political influence in Cuba. Castro therefore had to walk a domestic and international tightrope: he had to maintain Cuban independence, and his own authority, without alienating powerful domestic or international allies and without inadvertently empowering possible domestic challengers.

As a result of these imperatives, Castro drifted inexorably toward the Soviet Union; but he did so gingerly and always on his own terms. The concrete steps he took to reduce American influence certainly had the predictable effect of alienating the United States. American anger and suspicion, in turn, pushed him closer to Moscow. The process began almost immediately after he took power. In May 1959, Cuba passed an agrarian reform law, expropriating a certain amount of American-owned property, raising American ire. On February 6, 1960, Soviet First Deputy Premier Anastas I. Mikoyan traveled to Cuba with a trade exhibition, meeting Castro and signing a series of agreements that included, among other things, $100 million in credits to help reduce Cuban dependence on the American economy. These developments prompted Eisenhower to sign a National Security Council directive exploring options for Castro's ouster. On April 19, the first shipment of Soviet crude oil arrived in Cuba; and when two American-owned oil companies, Esso and Texaco, refused to refine it, Castro nationalized their refineries. Eisenhower responded by cutting the Cuban sugar quota by 95 percent. The Soviet Union stepped into the breach and announced that it would buy the sugar that the United States refused to take. In October, Cuba seized $1 billion worth of US assets. On December 19, Castro proclaimed Cuba's full solidarity with the socialist bloc. The CIA began planning for an exile invasion from Guatemala. As one of his last acts as president, Eisenhower severed diplomatic relations with Cuba.

Figure 1.2   Nikita Khrushchev embraces Castro at the Theresa Hotel, Harlem, New York City, September 1960

So went the spiral of hostility two-step. Cuba and the United States were headed for a showdown.

THE BAY OF PIGS AND OPERATION MONGOOSE

On Friday, January 20, 1961, John Fitzgerald Kennedy became the thirty-fifth president of the United States. From a platform spanning the East Front of the Capitol on that cold winter morning, Kennedy gave what has become one of the most famous inaugural addresses in American history. "Let every nation know, whether it wishes us well or ill," said Kennedy, "that we shall pay any price, bear any burden, meet any hardship, support any friend, oppose any foe, in order to assure the survival and the success of liberty."

Fidel Castro had joined the ranks of the foes, and Cuba was no doubt very much on Kennedy's mind when he uttered those famous words. The CIA was busily working on a variety of schemes to overthrow Castro and had briefed Kennedy on them prior to his taking the oath of office. Some of the schemes were notable more for their hilarity than for their likely success. The CIA's Technical Services Division (TSD), for example, considered spraying a chemical similar to lysergic acid diethylamide (LSD) in the radio station from which Castro frequently broadcast speeches, hoping he would babble incoherently and thus lose credibility. They also tried to lace a box of his favorite cigars with a mind-altering drug, hoping he would smoke one before going on the air. They tried contaminating another with botulinum toxin. They turned to the Florida mob in search of a hit man. Most entertainingly, they planned to dust Castro's shoes with depilatory salts one night when he left them outside his hotel room to be polished, hoping that, if his hair and beard fell out, he would lose his domestic appeal. Needless to say, none of these schemes bore fruit.

The CIA's most serious attempt to oust Castro was the infamous Bay of Pigs invasion, April 17–19, 1961. The original plan, hatched during the Eisenhower administration, was to train and equip a force of Cuban exiles in Central America and drop them into the Escambray Mountains to rally the Cuban people against their new dictator. The operation was flawed from the beginning, based as it was on faulty estimates of Castro's vulnerability and of the force required. Tinkering transformed a flawed plan into a hopeless one. CIA planners changed their minds about air dropping the exiles into the mountains, deciding to land them on the southern coast near Trinidad instead. At the last minute, they changed the landing site to Playa Girón, a flat, swampy area far from any mountains, affording no cover and no escape. They also cut so far back on the number of bombing runs that the small, poorly equipped exile air force would make that it failed to knock out Castro's air power. Surrounded by Castro's soldiers and pounded from the air, the exile army barely managed a beachhead. With the situation desperate, the CIA pleaded with Kennedy to authorize American air support. But at the last minute, Kennedy refused, and Castro's forces routed the invaders.[2]

Despite the CIA's efforts to mask the American role in the operation, it clearly had Washington's fingerprints all over it. Kennedy duly accepted public responsibility for the fiasco after the fact. It was the first and biggest setback of his presidency, and it dealt a blow both to his self-confidence and

---

2. There is disagreement about the exact toll, but the most reliable sources suggest 114 invaders died and 1,189 were captured. A few of those captured were executed as criminals, but most were later ransomed for medical and agricultural supplies.

to his reputation. But Kennedy had, in fact, inherited an impossible predicament from Eisenhower. Kennedy knew that using American forces to oust Castro would generate tremendous ill will in Latin America, where memories of American interventionism still burned. Kennedy would have been delighted to have Cuban exiles oust Castro on their own, but he and others (including the Pentagon) had serious doubts about the CIA's plan. Yet he could see no alternative to going through with it. If he pulled the plug on the operation, the exiles, in their fury, would blow its cover. This would alienate everyone. Conservatives would doubt all the more strongly Kennedy's resolve to combat communism. Liberals would be appalled to learn that he had even contemplated such a move. Latin Americans would question his commitment to sovereignty and nonintervention. Kennedy also feared that the Soviets would conclude that he was weak and that communists would be emboldened all through the hemisphere. The main lesson Kennedy drew from the fiasco was to be more skeptical of his own intelligence community in the future.

The Bay of Pigs disaster left the Kennedy administration with few options. One was to try to bring greater economic and diplomatic pressure on Cuba. Efforts in this direction met with mixed success but ultimately proved insufficient to destabilize the Castro regime. Few other countries were willing to sever relations with Cuba, and fewer still were willing to go along with the United States in attempting to impose a complete economic embargo. The high-water mark of the Kennedy administration's efforts in this direction came at Punta del Este in January 1962, when the OAS declared Castro's government incompatible with the inter-American system and imposed an arms embargo. Shortly thereafter, on February 3, Kennedy declared an American embargo on all trade with Cuba, except for critical medical supplies. But the Soviet Union and its client states were happy to fill the void.

This left one arrow in the American quiver other than a full-scale military attack: covert operations. But the record of anti-Castro covert operations to this point was one of dismal failure. To bring energy and coherence to it, Kennedy formed the Special Group (Augmented), or SGA, in November 1961.

The SGA packed tremendous political punch. Its members included Bobby Kennedy, Director of Central Intelligence John McCone, Special Assistant for National Security Policy McGeorge Bundy, Undersecretary of State U. Alexis Johnson, Deputy Secretary of Defense Roswell Gilpatric, Chairman of the Joint Chiefs of Staff (JCS) General Lyman Lemnitzer, and presidential military adviser General Maxwell Taylor. Secretary of State Dean Rusk and Secretary of Defense Robert S. McNamara attended meetings as well, though neither was officially a member.

In late 1961, the SGA concluded that efforts to topple Castro had to be centralized, coordinated, and placed under the day-to-day management of someone with the vision, energy, and skills to make things happen. The result was Operation Mongoose, and the SGA picked General Edward Lansdale to run it. Widely considered a genius at "special operations," Lansdale had extensive experience fighting communists in the Philippines and Vietnam during the 1950s and is thought by many to have inspired the character of Alden Pyle in Graham Greene's novel *The Quiet American*. A man of boundless energy and creativity, though also, as Thomas Powers would later recall, a man of "uneven judgment" occasionally taken with "nutty ideas," Lansdale threw himself wholeheartedly into any task he was given. From his office in the Pentagon, Lansdale worked furiously on a six-part plan for a massive program of sabotage, economic harassment, and psychological warfare designed to bring the Castro regime to its knees, coincidentally, by October 1962.

On February 20, 1962, Lansdale submitted his plan to the SGA for approval. Some were sympathetic to Lansdale's grandiose vision, but many had doubts. The group as a whole opted to begin more modestly. As a result, the first phase of Operation Mongoose—the spring and early summer of 1962— was restricted to intelligence collection, limited infiltrations and operations by Cuban exiles, economic sabotage, and exploratory psychological operations (mostly half-hearted efforts at propaganda broadcasts, easily jammed by the Castro regime). Mongoose accomplished little during this period, even though, in his report of July 25, 1962, Lansdale tried to sound upbeat about its prospects. But Lansdale's view was that much more could be done if the United States were "to provide maximum support of Cubans to liberate Cuba," so he called for aggressively stepped-up operations.

It was not entirely clear at the time exactly how much progress the White House did—or could—expect from Operation Mongoose. On the one hand, it lacked nothing in financial, human, and technical resources. Task Force W, a new unit of the CIA's covert operations branch under the direction of William Harvey, was created specifically to support Operation Mongoose. The CIA's Miami station—at that time the biggest CIA installation outside of headquarters at Langley—was one of the largest employers in the state of Florida. The Senate committee that in 1975–76 investigated American covert operations—the so-called Church Committee—estimated that as many as 12,000 agents were involved in anti-Castro activities in the early 1960s. The flotilla in Florida available to the CIA was said to be the third largest navy in the Western Hemisphere. On the other hand, CIA analysts had come to realize that the Bay of Pigs operation had been premised on a gross underestimation of Castro's domestic popularity. "The Castro regime has sufficient popular support and repressive capabilities," the CIA concluded just weeks before Operation Mongoose began, "to cope with any internal threat likely to develop within the foreseeable future." Few suspected that covert operations alone could topple the Castro regime. At some point, American military force might be required.

Operation Mongoose therefore proceeded in parallel with planning for military contingencies. Beginning in 1961, the US military began laying the groundwork for an air strike and invasion of Cuba. The air strike plan, OPLAN 312, called for more than 1,000 sorties against every aspect of Cuba's

---

HOW SERIOUS WAS OPERATION MONGOOSE?

Khrushchev and Castro saw Operation Mongoose as a serious attempt to trigger counterrevolution that heralded a decisive American military intervention in Cuba. Soviet and Cuban intelligence saw it as a half-hearted attempt to gather information and harass the Castro regime. How did Kennedy see it?

The available record suggests that Kennedy did not think Operation Mongoose was good for much. He certainly did not give Lansdale and Harvey free rein, and he did not energetically promote a coordinated effort between the CIA and the Pentagon to use covert operations to create a pretext for military action. In effect, he gave the covert action enthusiasts just enough leeway to enable them to feel as though they were doing something constructive and just enough to enable *him* to convince the hawks in the US government that he was serious about removing Castro. As McGeorge Bundy would later say, Operation Mongoose was "a psychological salve for inaction."

Others in the US government, however, were *very* serious about Operation Mongoose and very frustrated that it was not pursued as energetically as it might have been. Among those who would have liked to pursue covert operations more aggressively was the president's brother, Bobby.

---

military infrastructure, to soften up the island for a massive land invasion, laid out in detail in OPLAN 314.[3] These plans underwent various modifications as time went on, but they did not change in essential respects and represented the actual military options Kennedy had at his disposal during the Cuban missile crisis itself. Because Pentagon planners were thinking big, laying the groundwork for the kind of large-scale military action that would be needed to defeat a fully mobilized and determined Cuban resistance, Kennedy had neither small-scale nor flexible military options during the crisis itself.

THE SOVIET DECISION TO DEPLOY

The one thing that the Kennedy administration—indeed, the American people as a whole—feared most was that Castro would turn Cuba into a significant Soviet military outpost. Particularly worrisome was the prospect that Castro would allow the Soviet Union to deploy nuclear weapons on Cuban soil. This was also the one contingency capable of galvanizing Latin

---

3. "OPLAN" was Pentagon-speak for "Operational Plan." OPLAN 316 was a variant of OPLAN 314 that assumed a shorter time frame for preparation and implementation.

American support for Washington's hard-line position against the Cuban Revolution. In 1961 and early 1962, no one thought a nuclear deployment very likely. Though East bloc arms shipments to Cuba continued and even accelerated during this time, there was no intelligence to suggest that the Soviet Union and its allies were doing anything other than what they claimed: supplying Cuba with purely defensive weapons. So long as this was the case, the Kennedy administration could find little ground for complaint. Every country had the right to defend itself. It was also difficult to imagine that either Khrushchev or Castro would be so foolish. Surely, just about everyone in the Kennedy administration believed, Khrushchev would have to know that a nuclearized Cuba would provoke a political firestorm in the United States and that the president could not possibly stand for it. But this is precisely what Khrushchev did.

What did Khrushchev think he stood to gain by such a bold gamble? Or if there was nothing he thought he stood to *gain*, what did he think he might *avoid losing?* These questions have been the subject of endless debate by historians and, indeed, were great puzzles to the Kennedy administration itself once it discovered the missiles. There were several possibilities:

1. *Repairing the missile gap.* In the latter part of the 1950s, Khrushchev had made a great deal of an alleged Soviet superiority in strategic nuclear weapons. Events such as the 1957 launch of the *Sputnik* satellite and Yuri Gagarin's success in becoming the first human to orbit the earth in April 1961 seemed clearly to demonstrate Soviet leadership in rocket technology. All the while Khrushchev had boasted that the Soviet Union was producing long-range intercontinental ballistic missiles (ICBMs) "like sausages." The fear of falling behind the Soviet Union in nuclear missile capability prompted the United States to embark upon a desperate arms program of its own. Once American reconnaissance satellites finally managed to photograph the Soviet Union in detail, they discovered that the Soviets had a mere handful of ICBMs. What many had thought was a "missile gap" favoring the Soviet Union turned out to be a *massive* missile gap favoring the United States.

In October 1961, Deputy Secretary of Defense Roswell Gilpatric delivered a speech revealing that the US government knew about the real nuclear balance, thereby exposing Khrushchev's bluff. With insufficient ICBMs to redress the imbalance, Khrushchev's only hope for doing so quickly was to deploy medium-range and intermediate-range ballistic missiles (MRBMs and IRBMs) within striking distance of the United States. Cuba was the only friendly country that fit the bill.

2. *Defending Cuba.* The US government was clearly hostile to the Cuban Revolution. The Bay of Pigs, Operation Mongoose, the economic embargo, the Punta del Este meeting of the OAS, and increasingly visible military muscle-flexing in the Caribbean may all have suggested that the

United States would stop at nothing to destroy the Castro regime. With no hope of defending Cuba against a determined American assault by purely conventional military means, Khrushchev may have believed that only a local nuclear deterrent stood any chance of preventing an inevitable American attack.

3. *Berlin*. Khrushchev had utterly failed to get the Western powers to withdraw from Berlin, where they represented a major thorn in the side of the German Democratic Republic (GDR, East Germany) and an unwelcome outpost well behind the Iron Curtain. In June 1961, at a summit in Vienna, Khrushchev bullied Kennedy on the subject to no avail. The construction of the Berlin Wall, which began in August 1961, stanched the outflow of refugees from East to West through Berlin, solving an immediate demographic and economic problem and effectively protecting the East German currency. But the political and strategic problems remained. The Western presence in Berlin was a knife held at the throat of the GDR's legitimacy, an embarrassing beacon of Western values and Western lifestyles, and a potential military complication in the event of a war in central Europe. A deployment of nuclear missiles to Cuba might divert American attention from Berlin, split the NATO alliance, provoke the United States into taking some military action that would justify a Soviet seizure of West Berlin, or present the United States with a hemispheric threat serious enough to make them consider withdrawing from Berlin in return for Soviet concessions on Cuba.

4. *Missiles in Turkey*. As of May 1962, the United States had finished deploying Jupiter IRBMs in Turkey as part of its effort to extend its nuclear umbrella to its European NATO allies. Ironically, the Jupiter deployment was meant to counter what was perceived at the time to be a missile gap favoring the USSR. Vulnerable and unreliable, the Jupiters were quite worthless militarily, but they nonetheless irritated Khrushchev intensely, owing to their proximity to the Soviet Union. He may have conceived the Cuban deployment as a quid pro quo, or perhaps as a lever or bargaining chip to secure their withdrawal.[4]

5. *China*. Unity within the socialist bloc was breaking down as China began to assert itself and to criticize Khrushchev's unorthodoxy. He may have intended the deployment of missiles to Cuba as a way of demonstrating Soviet boldness and leadership in the global struggle against capitalism or as a way of preventing Cuba from drifting toward Chinese patronage, a possibility that seemed suddenly shockingly real in March 1962, when

---

4. Jupiter missiles were also deployed in Italy, and Thor missiles were deployed in Great Britain. These deployments also irritated Khrushchev, but the Turkish missiles drew most of his ire.

Figure 1.3 Kennedy and Khrushchev at the Vienna Summit, June 1961 (Courtesy John F. Kennedy Library)

Castro purged Aníbal Escalante and his pro-Soviet "micro-faction" because of Escalante's rising power and ambition.

6. *Cold War politics.* Khrushchev may have had a very general goal in mind: to put the United States on the geopolitical defensive, distract the Americans from Europe, impress non-aligned countries, and boost the morale of the Soviet bloc.

7. *Domestic politics.* Khrushchev was facing grumbling at home. His domestic program—particularly agricultural reform—was in shambles, and his foreign policy record was poor. He may have hoped that a bold foreign policy success would boost his domestic standing. Alternatively, he may have been pushed into the deployment by hard-liners.

A great deal depended on the Kennedy administration's ability to discern Khrushchev's motives. It would be difficult, when the crisis hit in October, to resolve it peacefully without knowing exactly what Khrushchev hoped to accomplish in the first place.

In his memoirs, Khrushchev wrote that his primary motive in deploying missiles to Cuba was to deter an American invasion. What we know about Khrushchev's deliberations suggests that this was indeed an important consideration. Khrushchev seems to have concluded from the Bay of Pigs operation that Kennedy was bent on destroying the Cuban Revolution. Operation Mongoose and Kennedy's energetic attempts to isolate Cuba economically and diplomatically seemed to Khrushchev to confirm this intention. Particularly important, it seems, was a conversation Kennedy had with Khrushchev's son-in-law, Aleksei Adzhubei, on January 30, 1962, in Washington. According to Soviet records of the meeting, Adzhubei reported that Kennedy had told him that he had criticized Allen Dulles after the Bay of Pigs operation. "I told him: you should learn from the Russians. When they had difficulties in Hungary, they liquidated the conflict in three days," Adzhubei reported Kennedy telling the beleaguered CIA director. "But you, Dulles, have never been capable of doing that." The Soviet Red Army had used overwhelming force to crush a nascent uprising in Hungary in 1956. Khrushchev seems to have drawn the obvious parallel.

Not only did Khrushchev believe that Kennedy had the *intention* to invade Cuba; he also knew, beyond the shadow of a doubt, that Kennedy had the *capability*. In March 1962, the United States carried out the largest and most complex military maneuvers in its history, LANTPHIBEX 1-62 and Operation Quick Kick, pointedly illustrating the US military's amphibious assault capabilities in the Caribbean. Khrushchev's own defense minister, Rodion Yakovlevich Malinovsky, had estimated that Cuba could withstand a determined American assault for a few days to a week. Losing Cuba would be a bitter blow to Khrushchev for many reasons, not least of which was his almost romantic attachment to Castro as a youthful revolutionary firebrand. As Sergo Mikoyan later put it, "Castro made Khrushchev feel like a young Bolshevik again." Racking his brains to find a way to protect Cuba from the inevitable American onslaught, Khrushchev was strongly attracted to the nuclear option.

But the nuclear option was not, in fact, Khrushchev's only alternative; and historians have often thought that if Khrushchev's sole motive had been to defend Cuba, he would have opted for something far less risky—perhaps a tripwire deployment of conventional Soviet forces configured for purely defensive operations. It would have been very difficult for the Kennedy administration to object to any form of Soviet–Cuban military cooperation so clearly intended for self-defense. A deployment completely lacking in power projection capability would have threatened no one. It also would have meant that if the United States attempted to destroy Castro militarily, it would inevitably also have to kill Soviet soldiers. A small conventional deployment would not have been able to thwart a determined American assault, but unless Kennedy was completely indifferent to the risks of escalation or retaliation elsewhere, it should have been sufficient to deter one. The fact that Khrushchev opted for a nuclear deployment instead of a purely conventional one has led many to suspect that he must have had some other motive in mind as well. And, indeed, in his memoirs, Khrushchev also notes that he was attracted to the deployment in part because it would have equalized "the balance of power."

Thus, it would appear that missile gap repair was on Khrushchev's mind as well. Whether this particular consideration was more or less important than the defense of Cuba is, at the end of the day, impossible to tell. Khrushchev certainly stressed the defense of Cuba motive, not only in his memoirs but also in Presidium meetings and in his communications with Castro; but this is hardly surprising as it would have been highly impolitic to foreground the selfish motive. The evidence suggests that Khrushchev cared deeply about both, and as there is no clear evidence that he ranked them in his own mind, it is simply impossible for us to know which, if either, was the stronger.

If we were to judge simply on the basis of the weight of evidence and testimony, we would have to conclude that these were the two main motives. But there is ample evidence that Jupiter missiles were also on

Figure 1.4 A Jupiter missile in Turkey (National Archives)

Khrushchev's mind, and the prospect of giving the Americans a dose of their own medicine filled him with glee. In April 1962, Malinovsky visited him at his *dacha* on the Black Sea coast, across from Turkey and the Jupiter sites, to brief him on the strategic nuclear balance and noted that the American missiles in Turkey had started to become operational. "Rodion Yakovlevich," Khrushchev inquired with a twinkle in his eye, "what if we throw a hedgehog down Uncle Sam's pants?"

There is probably merit also in the fifth, sixth, and seventh explanations. Quite apart from his romantic attachment to Castro's image, Khrushchev probably also cared about protecting Cuba—and being Cuba's unchallenged patron—because of the value this would have in deflecting China's increasingly vocal criticisms of Moscow. Repairing the missile gap, securing Cuba for the socialist bloc, and embarrassing Kennedy with a successful fait accompli all would have bolstered Soviet prestige and put the Americans on the defensive psychologically. And Khrushchev's growing body of critics at home would have had to have been impressed by such a bold, successful démarche. There is far less direct evidence of these considerations bearing on Khrushchev's deliberations than for the missile gap repair, defense of Cuba, and Turkish missile motivations, so it seems prudent to treat them as secondary; but Khrushchev's foremost biographer, William Taubman, makes a good case that Khrushchev was probably attracted to the idea for all of these reasons. "[T]he Cuban missiles were a cure-all," Taubman muses, but ultimately "a cure-all that cured nothing."

As far as we can tell, the decision to deploy nuclear missiles to Cuba was Khrushchev's alone, from start to finish. Khrushchev himself later claimed that it was a collective decision, arrived at by the Presidium as a whole only after careful deliberation. But this was a transparent effort to spread the blame for failure. The decision itself had Khrushchev's fingerprints all over it—and virtually no one else's. One thing now clear from Soviet records is that Khrushchev was at no stage pushed into anything.

The idea for the deployment appears first to have occurred to Khrushchev in late April 1962. The subject came up, at any rate, in conversations with First Deputy Premier Anastas Mikoyan and then shortly thereafter with Malinovsky on the Black Sea coast. Mikoyan had been the first high-level Soviet to visit Castro's Cuba and therefore knew Castro the longest. During a walk in Moscow's Lenin Hills, Khrushchev ruminated about the possibility of deploying strategic nuclear weapons to Cuba secretly and then informing Kennedy about them after the congressional elections in November. Kennedy, he believed, would accept the deployment much as the Soviet Union had accepted the deployment of Jupiter missiles in Turkey. Mikoyan was skeptical. He believed it likely that such a move would trigger a serious crisis. But he also knew that Castro would have to be consulted and thought it likely that Castro would object, so he did not press his skepticism at the time.

WAS THE CUBAN DEPLOYMENT ABOUT BERLIN?

When the United States discovered the deployment of nuclear missiles in October 1962, many American decision makers assumed that Khrushchev's gambit must have had something to do with Berlin. Berlin was very much on their minds at the time, so it was understandable that they thought it must have been on Khrushchev's mind as well. Indeed, prominent historians of the crisis continue to hold this view. Ernest May and Philip Zelikow, for example, write that

> What we now know indicates that Kennedy and his advisers understood the reasoning in the Kremlin better than have most scholars writing about the crisis in retrospect. While Khrushchev and his colleagues did indeed care a great deal about Cuba, the thought of deterring a US invasion figured only incidentally in their discussions about the missile deployments. Calculations about the strategic nuclear balance were much more in evidence. Berlin was an omnipresent and dominating concern.

There is, however, no testimony or documentary evidence suggesting that the deployment was about Berlin. To the contrary, both Khrushchev's son Sergei and his son-in-law Aleksei Adzhubei have insisted that he never linked the two issues. Moreover, circumstantial considerations cast doubt on the Berlin explanation. Berlin had been a problem for Khrushchev for years; if a Cuban deployment had been helpful, why did the idea only occur to him in the spring of 1962? More importantly, why did Khrushchev make no effort to exert pressure on Berlin during the crisis itself? And why did he never seek concessions on Berlin as a quid pro quo for withdrawing the missiles from Cuba? Of all the possible motives behind the deployment, the "Berlin gambit" explanation is by far the least plausible.

Khrushchev began building support for the idea in May, bringing into the discussion a small group who could be counted on either simply to defer to Khrushchev or to support the idea enthusiastically. These included Marshal S. S. Biryuzov and Secretary of the Central Committee Frol R. Kozlov. Kozlov was a political hack known mostly for his loyalty to Khrushchev. Biryuzov was the head of the Strategic Rocket Forces, the organization that stood most to gain institutionally from the deployment. Foreign Minister Andrei Gromyko was also brought into the discussion at this point. While he later claimed to have had doubts, there is no evidence Gromyko raised any serious objections.

Notably missing from the discussion was anyone with detailed knowledge of the United States, such as ambassador to Washington Anatoly Dobrynin or Khrushchev's special assistant for international affairs Oleg Troyanovsky, who grew up in Washington, D.C., attended the Friends School, spoke perfect English, and had a keen political eye. Nor did Khrushchev consult anyone in the Soviet intelligence community who followed American politics closely. There was no shortage of experts who might have warned Khrushchev that he was playing with fire, but Khrushchev did not ask.

It was at this point that Khrushchev decided to send a delegation to Cuba. To lay the groundwork properly, he decided he needed a more reliable point man in Havana than the current Soviet ambassador, Sergei Kudriavtsev, whose self-important pomposity did nothing but irritate the Cubans. The obvious man for the job was Aleksandr Alekseev, then in Havana under the cover of being a journalist, who spoke excellent Spanish and was on good personal terms with both Castro and Che. Alekseev traveled to Moscow to meet with Khrushchev and his ad hoc group, expecting straightforward instructions on how to play his new role. He was floored to learn that Khrushchev wanted to know how Castro would respond to an offer of Soviet nuclear missiles. Flustered, Alekseev bluntly stated that he doubted Castro would agree because he would expect an adverse reaction from other Latin American countries. But Khrushchev was clearly not interested in debate. He mounted a lengthy defense of the idea, stressing the overriding importance of deterring an American invasion of Cuba, and instructed Alekseev to prepare for Biryuzov's mission, which would also include alternate Presidium member Sharaf Rashidov, who had recently joined Khrushchev's inner group, to give it some political weight.

Khrushchev and Gromyko left Moscow for a state visit to Bulgaria during the week of May 14, while Biryuzov's team prepared. It was in Bulgaria, according to Khrushchev's memoirs, that "the idea of installing missiles with nuclear warheads in Cuba without letting the United States find out until it was too late to do anything about them" occurred to him for the first time. His speeches from that trip evince outrage at the American deployment of missiles in Turkey, so it is very likely that the idea for a Cuban deployment was on his mind—but this was not, in fact, where the idea first dawned on him. Gromyko would later claim that it was on the flight back home from Bulgaria that he first expressed serious reservations: "Putting missiles in Cuba would cause a political explosion in the United States," Gromyko recalled saying. While Khrushchev surprised Gromyko by not responding in a rage, it was clear that his mind was firmly made up to proceed.

Back in Moscow, Khrushchev convened the Defense Council and ordered detailed planning to begin. He instructed the council's secretary, Colonel General Semyon Ivanov, to craft a conceptual sketch of a plan to deploy nuclear weapons in Cuba. Three days later, at a combined meeting of the Defense Council and the Presidium, Malinovsky formally presented the plan, which Khrushchev enthusiastically endorsed. The culture of Soviet decision making was such that it was difficult for subordinates who harbored doubts to challenge the clear preference of the leader, and indeed no one did. But Khrushchev clearly sensed some unease because he took the unusual step of insisting that everyone affix his signature to the decision to proceed.

On May 27, the leader of the delegation to Cuba—Marshal Biryuzov—got his marching orders. Traveling pseudonymously under the guise of an agricultural mission, the group arrived in Havana with little fanfare on May 29. When Alekseev informed Raúl Castro that "Engineer Petrov" was actually Biryuzov, the Cubans knew something big was up and arranged a meeting with Castro right away. Castro listened to Biryuzov's proposal thoughtfully but did not immediately answer. According to Alekseev, Castro wanted to know if the purpose of the deployment was to bolster the global position of the socialist camp. Biryuzov replied that the purpose was to defend the Cuban Revolution. Castro consented, insisting that he was doing so only for the greater good of socialism. In reality, Biryuzov was more interested in the latter and Castro the former: he was eager to have in place the ultimate deterrent against *Yanqui* aggression. But it suited each other's pride to represent both the proposal and its acceptance as gestures of altruism. Work began immediately on a formal agreement.

There was a certain irony in the fact that the defense of Cuba figured so heavily both in Khrushchev's proposal and in Castro's acceptance—for neither Soviet nor Cuban intelligence considered an American attack likely at that time. The KGB (*Komitet Gosudarstvennoĭ Bezopasnosti*) inferred from the Bay of Pigs that Kennedy was a moderate, not a hawk. The intelligence the KGB received during and immediately after the operation suggested that it had been pushed upon a reluctant Kennedy by the CIA and other hard-line elements in the US government. His refusal to use American forces to finish the job suggested a disinclination to be aggressive. As far as we can tell from the available record and from the testimony of former officials, at no time between the Bay of Pigs and the decision to deploy missiles did Soviet intelligence warn that the danger of an American attack was growing.

According to the testimony from former Cuban intelligence analyst Domingo Amuchastegui,[5] Cuban intelligence also downplayed the danger of an American attack during this period. Particularly interesting, according to Amuchastegui, were the very perceptive inferences Cuban intelligence drew from Operation Mongoose, which seemed clearly designed merely to gather information and harass the Castro regime rather than to foment insurrection, provide diversions, or otherwise lay the groundwork for an American attack. Moreover, Cuban intelligence analysts firmly believed that Kennedy would not consider mounting military operations against Cuba without OAS support, which was something Kennedy could expect only in the event of some outrageous provocation—such as a deployment of Soviet nuclear missiles to Cuba.

Amuchastegui insists, however, that Soviet intelligence *did* sound the alarm over American intentions whenever the opportunity to invade presented itself.

---

5. Pronounced "a-mu-CHAS-te-gi."

If this is correct, it seems the KGB had concluded one thing but was reporting the opposite to its Cuban counterpart. One possible explanation for this
is that Soviet intelligence was attempting to persuade the Cubans to endorse
Khrushchev's nuclear proposal.

Castro, for his part, agreed with Khrushchev: *his* reading of the Bay of
Pigs was that it signaled unrelenting American hostility. Castro was convinced
that Kennedy would not be able to tolerate the humiliation of the Bay of Pigs
fiasco forever. Nor, in his view, would the United States tolerate a socialist
regime in what was, in effect, a former American colony right on America's
doorstep. Castro therefore accepted the assessments of the American threat
that Soviet intelligence disingenuously passed on to Cuban intelligence and
ignored the contrary assessments of his own intelligence community. In
none of the three principal countries, then, were political leaders interacting
constructively with their intelligence communities.

With Castro's agreement, the die was cast. The Soviet Union and the United
States were on a collision course over Soviet nuclear missiles in Cuba. None
of the three leaders expected this. Kennedy never imagined that Khrushchev
would be so reckless as to attempt to sneak what Americans would surely
interpret as "offensive" nuclear weapons into America's backyard. Kennedy
failed to imagine this because he knew what kind of reaction such a move
would provoke—and, knowing this, he mistakenly assumed Khrushchev would
know it, too. He failed to imagine it also because he did not understand the
various predicaments Khrushchev faced and he did not appreciate how
reckless and headstrong Khrushchev could be once an idea took hold of him.
Kennedy failed to appreciate (though of course he could not control) the lessons
Khrushchev and Castro drew from the Bay of Pigs; Operation Mongoose;
attempts to isolate Cuba diplomatically, economically, and politically; and osten-
tatious displays of US military might in the Caribbean—displays intended
primarily, ironically, to *deter* precisely the kind of reckless adventurism that
a Soviet deployment of nuclear missiles to Cuba would represent. Kennedy,
in short, utterly lacked empathy with his adversaries. As a result, he took no
timely steps to communicate clearly either his unwillingness to tolerate such
a deployment or to find a way to live with the Castro regime.

Khrushchev fared no better. Boxed in, blinkered, and badly advised,
Khrushchev made no serious effort to understand how Kennedy would react
to his gambit. He overestimated how much weight the technical legality of
the deployment, and its symmetry (as he saw it) with American missile
deployments in Turkey, would carry with both Kennedy and the international
community. He failed to see that by attempting to sneak missiles into Cuba,
others would conclude that his intentions were offensive and aggressive, rather
than largely defensive, or that they were driven by a sense of need rather
than a perception of opportunity. He might have been able to avoid these
misperceptions and to understand Kennedy's perspective if he had subjected
his idea to serious scrutiny and, in particular, if he had made good use of

the expertise available to him. But instead he silenced his only skeptics and surrounded himself with yes-men and incompetents (Biryuzov returned from Cuba convinced, for example, that strategic nuclear missiles could easily be disguised as palm trees).

Like Khrushchev, Castro misperceived American intentions, failed to think through the likely implications of the deployment, and ignored his best available advice. His complicity with Khrushchev was downright cavalier. It seems likely that he failed to subject the idea to serious critical scrutiny in part because it had a compelling emotional appeal: with Soviet nuclear weapons operational on Cuban soil, Castro believed, Cuba would, for the first time in its history, stand on a plane with its nemesis, the United States of America. The deployment so gratified his pride, offering such an opportunity to redeem Cuba's long-standing historical humiliation, that he simply found it irresistible.

Thus, all three leaders stumbled into the Cuban missile crisis in large part because of what social scientists have come to call "mirror-imaging." All three were acting on the basis of perceptions and judgments deeply informed by their own historical perspectives and experiences. All three were oblivious to their counterparts' radically different perspectives and experiences. All three assumed that others saw, or would see, the world the same way they did, so all three miscalculated the consequences of their own actions. Sometimes it is possible to correct for these failings, but it is almost impossible to do so without being willing to subject one's views to serious scrutiny. None of the three leaders was open to information challenging prior beliefs. None looked for it, and if they encountered it at all, they found ways to dismiss it or ignore it. In a very profound way, in other words, the Cuban missile crisis was a colossal mistake—one for which the world very nearly paid the ultimate price.

CHAPTER 2

Deployment and Discovery

THE SOVIET UNION had never attempted a major military deployment by sea, let alone to the other side of the world—and in secret. The challenge was a formidable one. It would require meticulous planning, watertight security, and flawless execution. If there is one thing that a professional soldier knows, it is that nothing goes exactly as planned. And in this case, it did not. But it is remarkable how nearly it did.

The code name for the deployment was Operation Anadyr, a label chosen primarily for its deceptive value. Anadyr was the name of a river in the northeastern USSR that flowed into the Bering Sea. Soviet planners hoped that if the code name became known to Western intelligence, they might assume that the operation had something to do with the Arctic rather than with the Caribbean. And to enhance that likelihood, Soviet commanders did not tell troops bound for Cuba their true destination and ordered them to bring full winter gear. The idea was that if a soldier or a sailor let slip that he was shipping out, he would probably give the impression to his friends, family, or eavesdropping Western spies that he was headed north, not south. Such was the care with which Soviet planners attempted to maintain secrecy.

Responsibility for planning Operation Anadyr lay with the General Staff Main Operations Directorate, headed by the same General Ivanov who served as secretary to the Defense Council. Much of the work fell to his deputy, General Anatoly Ivanovich Gribkov. As Gribkov tells in fascinating detail in his memoir of the crisis, he literally spent weeks writing and rewriting plans and orders by hand, racking his brains to try to anticipate every possible security flaw, frantically trying to master the complex logistics of redeploying units and weapons already on duty in various places in the Soviet Union, even familiarizing himself with the intricacies of international law so that he could help draft the Soviet–Cuban treaty governing the deployment.

DETAILS OF THE DEPLOYMENT

Since the deployment had more than one purpose, it required a variety of forces. To defend Cuba against a possible American assault, it was necessary to send a full combined-arms, battle-capable force. Given the enormous numerical and logistical advantages the US military would enjoy in a determined attack on Cuba, the Soviet troops sent to defend Cuba would have to be self-sufficient and would have to compensate somehow for their numerical inferiority. The only way to do this, Soviet planners surmised, was to equip them with tactical nuclear weapons—short-range weapons designed not to destroy cities or distant military targets but to kill large numbers of invading troops as they approached or hit the beaches.

To redress the strategic nuclear imbalance, it was necessary to send missiles capable of striking deep into the American heartland. The nuclear weapons these missiles would carry would be much more powerful than the tactical nuclear weapons and *would* be capable of destroying entire cities. To protect these missiles and their nuclear warheads, it was necessary to send significant numbers of supporting troops and equipment.

To prevent premature discovery of the deployment and to defend against American air attack and invasion, it was necessary to send sophisticated jet fighters and surface to air missiles (SAMs). These systems, too, required considerable numbers of supporting troops and equipment.

All told, Operation Anadyr called for the deployment of approximately 50,000 Soviet soldiers, sailors, and airmen. To transport them and their equipment would require 85 ships, many of which would make several round-trip journeys. Khrushchev's goal was to announce the deployment publicly at the United Nations (UN) in November, right after the US midterm congressional elections, giving the Soviet military just four months to achieve operational readiness in Cuba.

Despite the intensive planning effort, to some extent the Soviets made things up as they went along or did things for the sake of speed that made little military sense. To help protect against premature American discovery, for example, it would have been wise first to deploy a robust antiaircraft capability in Cuba built around the Soviet Union's newest and best SAM, the S-75, which had proven itself capable of knocking out the high-altitude U-2 reconnaissance plane (an S-75 battery near Smolensk had downed Francis Gary Powers' U-2 on May Day, 1960). Indeed, the Soviets had authorized S-75 deployments to Cuba even before planning for Anadyr got under way—in April 1962—diverting missiles originally earmarked for Egypt. Yet the original Anadyr plan gave the MRBM deployment priority. When Khrushchev decided in July that it would be better to have the SAM system in place first, shipping schedules had to be juggled to accommodate the change; and the SAM deployment was still only partially complete when the strategic missiles began to arrive in Cuba in September.

The original Anadyr plan called also for only one type of tactical nuclear weapons system, the coastal-defense FKR-1 (*Frontovaya Krylaya Raketa*) cruise missile. But in September, when Khrushchev began to fear premature American discovery and an aggressive American reaction, the Soviets rushed mobile Luna tactical nuclear missiles to Cuba, as well as nuclear bombs for Il-28 jet light bombers. These systems had no immediate deterrent value because the Soviets never informed the Americans of their presence. While the United States detected some of these "dual-use" (conventional or nuclear) delivery systems, American intelligence did not know they had actually been supplied with nuclear weapons.

The original plan, finally, also included a robust naval force, but the naval deployment was canceled late in the game, for fear of being too provocative. In its stead, the Soviet navy sent four Foxtrot-class diesel-electric submarines into the western Atlantic, each equipped with a single nuclear torpedo in addition to its complement of conventional torpedoes, in case, if a shooting war broke out, an American aircraft carrier group presented itself as a target.

At the end of the day, then, what the Soviets deployed to Cuba and how they deployed it mapped only imperfectly onto the original Anadyr plan. Nonetheless, what the Soviets eventually deployed to Cuba composed a lengthy list:

Strategic nuclear weapons

• Thirty-six R-12 MRBMs (NATO designation SS-4 "Sandal") in three regiments of 12. Each regiment had eight launchers, for a total of 24 (the idea was that some launchers would fire more than one missile). There were also six "dummy" or "practice" R-12s. The yield of the warheads these missiles carried has variously been reported to range from 200 kilotons to 1 megaton or more, or at least 15 to 70 times as powerful as the atomic bomb that destroyed Hiroshima during World War II (the larger estimate seems more likely). The R-12 missile had a range between 1,100 and 1,300 miles and from Cuban bases could hit targets as far away as New York, Chicago, and Dallas, as well as points in Latin America.

• Twenty-four R-14 IRBMs (NATO designation SS-5 "Skean") in two regiments of 12 with a total of 16 launchers and warheads similar in yield to those provided for the R-12s. The R-14s never reached Cuba, although some of their warheads did, weathering the crisis aboard the *Aleksandrovsk* in the port of La Isabela throughout. The range of the R-14 was between 2,200 and 2,800 miles, meaning that if these missiles had become operational, they could conceivably have struck all, or very nearly all, of the lower 48 states of the United States, much of Canada, and much of Latin America.

Ground forces

• Four reinforced motorized rifle regiments, each of which had approximately 3,500 soldiers, for a total of 14,000. Although these were not heavy

Figure 2.1 Soviet R-12 (NATO designation SS-4) missile (Photo by Don Munton)

armored units, they did have a full range of equipment, including tanks, artillery, and antitank missiles.

• Six Luna (NATO designation "FROG," for "Free Rocket Over Ground") missiles, in three detachments of two launchers and two missiles each. Each detachment had three nuclear warheads, for a total of nine; and each warhead had a yield of approximately 2 kilotons. The Luna was a short-range (40 mile), unguided battlefield rocket, similar to the American "Honest John," useful primarily against large concentrations of enemy forces. Khrushchev decided to add nuclear-armed Lunas to the deployment mix only in September 1962.

Air and air defense forces
• Forty-two Il-28 (NATO designation "Beagle") jet light bombers, of which six were specially fitted to carry an 8–12-kiloton nuclear bomb. The Il-28 was an obsolete, subsonic aircraft with a range of just 600 miles but still capable of striking targets in the southeastern United States.

• Forty MiG-21 (NATO designation "Fishbed") fighters—at the time, among the most advanced fighter aircraft in the Soviet inventory.

• Seventy-two S-75 launchers (NATO designation SA-2), with a total of 144 antiaircraft missiles.

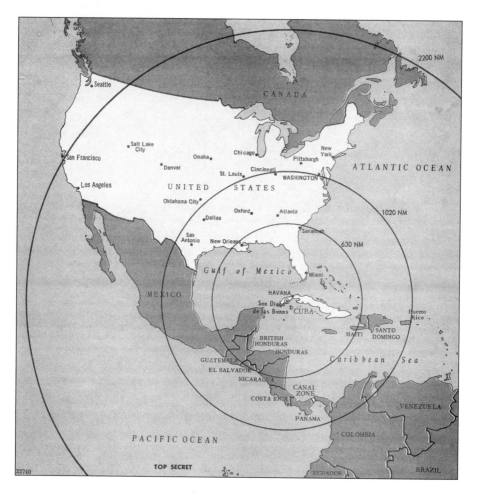

Figure 2.2 CIA estimates of II-28, R-12 missile, and R-14 missile ranges (Courtesy John F. Kennedy Library)

Coastal defense forces

• Eighty FKR-1 cruise missiles (NATO designation SSC-2 "Salish") in two regiments with eight launchers each, five missiles per launcher, and five 5- to 12-kiloton warheads per launcher. The FKR-1 had a range of 125 miles.

• Thirty-two S-2 "Sopka" (NATO designation SSC-2 "Samlet") missiles at four fixed cruise missile sites, with two launchers each, with a range of 50 miles and conventional high-explosive warheads.

• Twelve Komar patrol boats, each with two launchers for conventionally armed missiles with a 25-mile range.

As we mentioned, the original plan had also called for significant naval forces, including a squadron of 11 submarines and a squadron of surface ships (two cruisers, two missile-firing destroyers, two regular destroyers, 16 torpedo boats, two supply ships, two tankers, two bulk carriers, and one repair ship, as well as four atomic mines, to protect the fleet). These were ultimately not deployed. Eliminating the planned naval deployment in September meant that the total number of Soviet military personnel sent to Cuba would also drop, to 45,234, of which 3,332—as well as the R-14 missiles—were on the high seas when Kennedy imposed the quarantine.

In addition to planning what forces to send to Cuba, the Soviet leadership had to consider the issue of command. Khrushchev played an active role in this and exercised generally poor judgment. A serious error was his appointment of General Issa Pliyev as commander-in-chief of the Soviet Group of Forces in Cuba. Pliyev was famous for having led the last cavalry charge in history, and he was a highly decorated soldier with excellent standing among his troops and fellow officers. Khrushchev selected him over the General Staff's recommendation, partly because he was tough-minded and loyal but also partly because, should his identity become known, he would be less likely to arouse suspicions about the nature or purpose of the deployment than would an officer from the Strategic Rocket Forces. But Pliyev lacked tact and subtlety, behaved in a haughty way, and never established good working relationships either with his principal deputy or with Fidel Castro. The result was a good deal of unnecessary friction within the Soviet command and between the Soviet military in Cuba and their hosts.

Khrushchev was inclined to entrust Pliyev with the authority to use the tactical nuclear weapons under his command in the event of an American invasion (Khrushchev was very clear from the beginning that the strategic nuclear weapons in Cuba could only be used upon order from Moscow). As Gribkov recalls, Khrushchev gave Pliyev his instructions orally in July and confirmed them in writing in September, but Malinovsky neither signed nor transmitted the written confirmation, on the ground that doing so was superfluous. During the crisis itself, Khrushchev rescinded the authority he had predelegated, categorically forbidding any use of nuclear weapons without Moscow's express permission. But in 1962 there were no physical means to ensure these weapons could not be used without proper authority, and Pliyev was precisely the kind of egotistical, headstrong commander who would resent a diminution of his authority and who would be tempted to use whatever means were available for his defense if communications with Moscow were cut and he felt that the alternative was the annihilation of his forces. A veteran of Stalingrad, among many other battles, Pliyev did not shy away from bloodshed.

Arrangements also had to be made concerning the rights, responsibilities, and obligations of both Cuba and the Soviet Union now that the two countries were embarking on such an unprecedentedly bold and far-reaching project in military cooperation. To that end, Raúl Castro traveled to Moscow in early July to negotiate a formal treaty. Originally called the Treaty Between the Government of the Republic of Cuba and the Government of the Union of Soviet Socialist Republics on the Stationing of Soviet Armed Forces on the

Territory of the Republic of Cuba, the text Raúl carried back to Cuba for Fidel's approval gave the Soviet Union control over the weapons and personnel deployed to Cuba, other than weapons formally to be transferred to the Cuban Armed Forces, but obliged Soviet forces to observe Cuban laws and granted only temporary use of Cuban territory. The treaty was to remain in effect initially for five years and was renewable but could be terminated by either party on one year's notice. In the event the agreement was terminated, any fixed installations and equipment the Soviet Union left behind would become Cuban property. Castro proposed a number of refinements to the title and the text of the treaty, primarily intended to emphasize the defensive purposes of the deployment, and dispatched Che Guevara and Emilio Aragonés to Moscow in August to secure Khrushchev's agreement. Among other things, at this time the Cubans proposed going public with the agreement, to forestall an adverse reaction should the United States discover the deployment prematurely; but Khrushchev refused, insisting that there was no need. The final version of the document bore the title Treaty Between the Government of the Republic of Cuba and the Government of the Union of the Soviet Socialist Republics on Military Cooperation for the Defense of the National Territory of Cuba in Case of Aggression, so as to stress the defensive nature of the operation.

WHAT WOULD HAVE HAPPENED IF KHRUSHCHEV HAD GONE PUBLIC WITH THE DEPLOYMENT?

Critics of Khrushchev's decision making often claim that he erred by not going public with the nuclear deployment to Cuba, as Castro urged him to do, via Che and Aragonés, in late August. The deployment was perfectly legal under international law. Had he announced it publicly, he would have been able to stress its symmetry with the American Jupiter deployment in Turkey and he would have undercut the charge that secrecy and deception indicated nefarious intent. In short, Khrushchev would have been in a much better position in the battle for global public opinion. As senior members of the Kennedy administration candidly admitted years after the crisis, a public deployment would have been much more difficult for the Kennedy administration to oppose.

It is far from clear, however, that going public with the deployment would have guaranteed its success. The outcry in the United States (and in Latin America) would have been severe in any case, and Kennedy would have opposed it energetically. There would have been calls for immediate decisive action to oust Castro. Khrushchev felt that Kennedy would be vulnerable to this pressure to act and, thus, that the risks of going public outweighed the benefits. Since there is no way of knowing whether Khrushchev's assessment of the risks and benefits was correct, there is no way of knowing whether his failure to go public with the deployment was a mistake.

The Soviets were in a hurry and did not wait. By the middle of July they began shipping men and equipment. The *Maria Ulyanov* arrived in the port of Cabañas on July 26. This was the first of approximately 150 trips, each of which took place under a painstaking veil of secrecy. Officers, crews, and passengers were not permitted to communicate with the outside world once loading began. Captains of ships would not discover their destinations until well out at sea, where they were instructed to open sealed envelopes in the presence of political officers. Much of the loading and unloading took place at night, and any equipment identifiable from the air had to be carefully shrouded or crated. While at sea, Soviet soldiers were not allowed out on deck during daylight and had to suffer brutally hot and cramped conditions inside. Many fell ill; some died and were buried at sea. A lucky few who traveled to Cuba in the relative comfort of a passenger liner were instructed, as they approached Cuba, to go out on deck, play guitar, snap photographs, and otherwise look like tourists for the benefit of passing American reconnaissance planes.

Once in Cuba, Soviet soldiers moved out from port by night and did their best to stay out of sight of the Cuban population. But Cuba was a small place,

Figure 2.3   Soviet ship *Poltava* en route to Cuba (Courtesy John F. Kennedy Library)

and the roads on which Soviet troops and equipment traveled to their destinations passed through towns and villages; thus, it was impossible for the locals not to notice them—particularly when, even though disguised as civilians wearing plaid shirts, large numbers of clean-cut, physically fit young men formed up in ranks and marched to and from transport trucks. In Cuba, Anadyr quickly became known as Operation Checkered Shirt.

THE INTELLIGENCE GAME OF CAT AND MOUSE

American intelligence noticed the dramatic spike in shipping traffic right away and strove to discern its meaning. To do so, it turned to all three of its principal sources of information: photo intelligence (PHOTINT), supplied primarily by aerial reconnaissance; human intelligence (HUMINT), supplied primarily by Cuban refugees and operatives in various other places where the movements of Soviet ships could be observed (not only in Cuba but also in such places as the Strait of Gibraltar or the Bosporus, through which Soviet ships from the Black Sea had to pass); and signals intelligence (SIGINT), which relied primarily upon the interception and attempted decryption of Soviet radio traffic. We know a good deal today about the contribution of PHOTINT and HUMINT to the handling of the Cuban missile crisis, but details on the SIGINT effort remain largely classified. It is known that SIGINT helped track both Soviet shipping to Cuba and the installation of radar systems on the island, despite the precautions the Soviets took to avoid relying on electronic communications.

The CIA was not the only organization collecting and processing intelligence. Both the US military and the State Department had their own in-house analysts, and these were also carefully following developments in Cuba. But the CIA took the lead role, and Director of Central Intelligence (DCI) John McCone was the chief spokesman for the intelligence community. The CIA concluded toward the end of August that between 4,000 and 6,000 Soviet personnel had arrived in Cuba since the beginning of July—a significant underestimate. Many were known to be technicians, but some were suspected to be military, even though no organized military units were identified. Large, mysterious crates were being unloaded from Cuban ports under cover of darkness and obviously heavy security, but US intelligence could not determine what they contained. The CIA did determine that the Soviets had installed sophisticated electronic and radar equipment in Cuba, and a high-altitude U-2 flight on August 29 revealed the construction of SAM sites as well as the presence of missile boats and various other land armaments.

It was the greatest fear of American leaders that the Soviets might be attempting to deploy strategic missiles, but virtually no one thought they would be so foolish. McCone was an exception. He had difficulty imagining why the Soviets would deploy an extensive air defense network in Cuba if not to protect nuclear missiles. McCone was correct but was jumping to conclusions.

There were many good reasons why a country as vulnerable as Cuba would want to try to blunt its adversary's massive aerial superiority. In Washington in August, and again from his honeymoon in France in early September, McCone urged more and more aggressive aerial reconnaissance and consistently sounded the alarm about the nuclear missile threat.

Meanwhile, worrying reports from Cuban refugees and operatives were pouring in. The difficulty with these reports was that they were almost entirely unreliable. Refugees often told debriefers what they thought they wanted to hear. Untrained observers, or those unfamiliar with military equipment or procedures, did not know what they were seeing and often misremembered or mischaracterized it. A later postmortem showed that almost all of the 3,500 agent and refugee reports of missile sightings in Cuba over a two-year period were invalid and that perhaps as few as eight of 1,000 received in September and October 1962 had any basis in fact. The extremely low wheat-to-chaff ratio made it difficult to know exactly what was going on, and not surprisingly, these reports garnered little attention.

The most reliable source of information was photography. Pictures do not lie. And in the U-2, the United States had one of the most capable photography platforms imaginable. From an altitude well over 60,000 feet, immune to all but the Soviets' very latest SAM, the U-2 could take photographs of resolution sufficient to identify particular models of vehicles. U-2 photographs would ultimately provide the first hard proof of nuclear missile deployments in Cuba but not until October 15. There were two flights in August, on the 5th and 29th, and one on September 5; but the missile deployment was not far enough along to have been discovered at this point. The embarrassment of having a U-2 stray over Sakhalin Island on August 30 and the loss of another over Chinese territory on September 10 made the Kennedy administration skittish about authorizing too many flights over Cuba both because of the international outrage that would follow another such incident over Cuban territory and because SIGINT had determined that some of the SAM batteries were now operational. So the White House authorized only a limited number of flights along the periphery of Cuba or dipping only briefly into Cuban airspace, some of which were delayed by bad weather. These timid flights proved highly unsatisfactory.

The Soviets, meanwhile, were trying to complete the deployment undetected. They were not trying as hard as they might, however. Missile trailers too long to navigate corners on Cuban roads left telltale trails of downed telephone poles. Measures to disguise missile sites were unimaginative and inadequate. Launch pads, support buildings, and access roads were laid out in patterns typical of missile bases in the Soviet Union. While the strategic nuclear missiles themselves were always kept shrouded, the shrouds were so perfectly well fitted that their dimensions would give away what they were hiding if photographed from above. Various specialized pieces of supporting equipment, such as missile fueling trucks, were parked in open fields. And just as the White House feared authorizing reconnaissance flights because they

COULD THE UNITED STATES HAVE DISCOVERED THE MISSILES EARLIER?

Many have faulted the US intelligence community for failing to discover the deployment of the missiles until they were almost operational. Critics stress in particular the timidity of the U-2 reconnaissance program in Cuba as well as the CIA's disdain for eyewitness reports from Cuban refugees.

With respect to U-2 reconnaissance, it is an open question whether a more active program would have turned up decisive evidence earlier than mid-October in any case. Construction at missile bases was not far enough along in September to yield obvious clues about their nature or purpose. The Soviets were making efforts to mask the deployment, and these efforts were largely successful. Bad weather in the Caribbean during hurricane season also restricted opportunities for aerial photography. It is conceivable that the first mission that actually returned with decisive evidence was the first mission that would have been able to do so. It is, however, ironic that Kennedy—who was so eager to know what the Soviets were doing in Cuba—held back the U-2 out of fear that one might be shot down just as Khrushchev was ordering his air defense forces to hold their fire. Each, in a sense, was unwittingly making the other's life easier.

The CIA was indeed skeptical of eyewitness reports but very often for good reasons. Again, it is difficult to know whether giving these reports more credit would have led to an earlier discovery. Intelligence assessment is an enormously difficult task, and public opinion typically overestimates what intelligence communities know and can do. At the end of the day, the CIA managed to alert the president to the Soviet deployment in time for him to formulate a response, and this must count as a significant intelligence success.

might prove to be provocative, the Soviets refused to authorize the use of their sophisticated SAMs against the few U-2 flights the White House *did* authorize, out of fear that shooting one down would provoke the United States.

WARNINGS TOO LATE

Though Kennedy did not yet have any hard information suggesting that the Soviets were deploying nuclear weapons to Cuba, he decided that he should start sending signals that he would not tolerate it if they did.

In part, disturbing reports of the sudden massive increase in Soviet shipments to Cuba prompted Kennedy's decision to make deterrent threats. But so also did domestic and governmental pressures. Lansdale had begun pushing for real action on Mongoose, and his supporters in the administration were lobbying for more forceful action against Castro. Some, such as McCone, had become convinced that covert action would not be enough and were lobbying for stepped-up preparation of military contingencies. Republicans started making Cuba an issue as the midterm congressional election campaign began. All of this put Kennedy in a bind. He did not want to look weak or indifferent, but neither did he want to be provocative. What he wanted, most of all, was simply that nothing bad happen.

On August 31, Senator Kenneth Keating (R-NY) charged the Kennedy administration with willful negligence on Cuba. This was the first of 25 public statements Keating would make over a two-month period alleging that the White House was asleep at the wheel. Citing unnamed sources, Keating claimed that the Soviets had deployed more than 1,000 troops in Cuba, and he also claimed that they were building missile bases. Though he refused to identify his sources, Keating insisted that they were reliable; and the energy with which he pressed his case quickly made him the administration's most effective and most irksome critic.[1] But Keating's was just one voice among many. Prominent senators such as Homer Capehart (R-IN), Barry Goldwater (R-AZ), Karl Mundt (R-SD), and John Tower (R-TX) charged Kennedy with weakness and lobbied for action ranging from blockade to invasion. So also did former vice president and current California gubernatorial candidate Richard Nixon.

On September 4, Kennedy invited a congressional delegation to a detailed briefing on the intelligence on Cuba. Although there was ample evidence of a major Soviet military buildup, Kennedy insisted that everything the United States had been able to observe up until this point was defensive in character. There was no hard evidence of missiles or missile bases or indeed of any other weapons systems that posed a threat to American soil. Shortly after the briefing, Press Secretary Pierre Salinger read the following statement on Kennedy's behalf:

> All Americans, as well as all of our friends in this Hemisphere, have been concerned over the recent moves of the Soviet Union to bolster the military power of the Castro regime in Cuba. Information has reached this Government in the last four days from a variety of sources which establishes without doubt that the Soviets have provided the Cuban Government with a number of anti-aircraft defense missiles with a slant range of twenty-five miles which are similar to early models of our Nike. Along with these missiles, the Soviets are apparently providing the extensive radar and other electronic equipment which is required for their operation. We can also confirm the presence of several Soviet-made motor torpedo boats carrying ship-to-ship guided missiles having a range of fifteen miles. The number of Soviet military technicians now known to be in Cuba or en route—approximately 3,500—is consistent with

---

1. It now appears that Keating's source was Clare Boothe Luce, the prominent conservative Republican and former editor of *Vanity Fair*. Luce was apparently parroting sources in the Cuban exile community.

assistance in setting up and learning to use this equipment. As I stated last week, we shall continue to make information available as fast as it is obtained and properly verified.

There is no evidence of any organized combat force in Cuba from any Soviet bloc country; of military bases provided to Russia; of a violation of the 1934 treaty relating to Guantanamo; of the presence of offensive ground-to-ground missiles; or of other significant offensive capability either in Cuban hands or under Soviet direction and guidance. Were it to be otherwise, the gravest issues would arise . . .

To underscore his seriousness, three days later Kennedy asked Congress for authority to call up 15,000 reservists. Four days after that, Kennedy made another public statement. "If at any time the Communist build-up in Cuba were to endanger or interfere with our security in any way," he said, or if Cuba were to "become an offensive military base of significant capacity for the Soviet Union," then the United States would "do whatever must be done to protect its own security and that of its allies."

Kennedy clearly hoped his words and deeds would convince Americans that he was on top of the problem. He wanted to reassure them, too, that while there was as yet no indication that the Soviet Union was turning Cuba into an offensive military outpost, he would not allow them to do so if they tried. He was, in short, displaying good political instincts.

Was he simply talking tough for domestic political purposes? Or was he also trying to deter Khrushchev? Probably both to some extent. What *is* clear is that Kennedy did not want Soviet nuclear missiles in Cuba. During a meeting at the White House on August 23 called to discuss McCone's concerns, Kennedy had said bluntly that he would not tolerate the presence of Soviet missiles in Cuba. If necessary, he would use force to remove them. But if he really thought there was any danger that the Soviets would try to deploy missiles to Cuba, he should have started dissuading them right away. Why wait two weeks?

It is important to bear in mind that neither Kennedy nor virtually anyone else inside the administration *except* McCone thought the Soviets would attempt such a deployment. The prevailing view in the intelligence community, shared by Kennedy and others, was that expressed in the CIA's Special National Intelligence Estimate issued on September 19 (SNIE 85-3-62, "The Military Buildup in Cuba"). While noting that a deployment of strategic nuclear missiles would confer upon the Soviet Union a "considerable military advantage," the CIA insisted that such a move would be "incompatible with Soviet practice to date and with Soviet policy as we presently estimate it." So convinced was the CIA of its analysis that acting director Lieutenant General Marshall S. Carter and other senior officials in the intelligence community approved it without dissent—despite the fact that they knew that their honeymooning director disagreed wholeheartedly.

Years later, in March 1987, Kennedy's close friend and special counsel Theodore Sorensen made the following rather bold claim:

I believe the President drew the line precisely where he thought the Soviets were not and would not be; that is to say, if we had known that the Soviets were putting forty missiles in Cuba, we might under this hypothesis have drawn the line at 100, and said with great fanfare that we would absolutely not tolerate the presence of more than 100 missiles in Cuba. I say that believing very strongly that that would have been an act of prudence, not weakness. But I am suggesting that one reason the line was drawn at zero was because we simply thought the Soviets weren't going to deploy any there anyway.

Given the political explosiveness of *any* Soviet strategic nuclear weapons in Cuba, Sorensen's claim that Kennedy might have publicly accepted some is difficult to take at face value. But Sorensen seems entirely right that Kennedy did not expect missiles in Cuba anyway.

Thus, it seems clear that Kennedy's statements were intended at least in part—probably in large part—for domestic consumption. It is conceivable, however, that Kennedy had some lingering fear that Khrushchev might try after all to do something as seemingly risky as deploying nuclear missiles to Cuba, and hence it is conceivable that he sincerely hoped his statements would reduce this (small) likelihood further. In any case, his efforts were far too little, far too late.

Kennedy could not deter Khrushchev since the R-12 missiles had by then almost reached Cuba, but he did succeed in rattling him. Was Kennedy being pushed into taking a hard line? Were the hawks in Washington gaining the upper hand? Was Kennedy feeling pressure to act? Would this mean that if he discovered the deployment before it was complete, he would *not* take it in stride, as Khrushchev had initially calculated (or hoped)?

Khrushchev suddenly sensed danger. If the Americans discovered the deployment, they might swoop down upon Cuba before the Soviets could prevent an attack. He therefore practiced a little deterrence of his own. On September 21, in a speech to the UN, Foreign Minister Andrei Gromyko warned that an attack on Cuba would mean war with the Soviet Union. Leonid Brezhnev repeated the point a week later in Yugoslavia. But Khrushchev did not feel that words would be enough. What was needed, he decided, was a military stopgap: additional weapons that could hold an American invasion at bay.

Kennedy's sudden hard line therefore prompted Khrushchev to rush additional tactical nuclear weapons to Cuba. If the Soviet forces in Cuba had to defend themselves, their only hope of putting up a successful defense was to destroy large concentrations of American troops as they tried to come ashore. In a panic, Khrushchev asked Malinovsky to find out whether tactical nuclear weapons could be rushed to Cuba by air. The answer was yes but with great difficulty and unacceptable risks of discovery. Soviet aircraft in 1962 could not reach Cuba nonstop; they had to refuel, and even the friendliest refueling point—Conakry, Guinea—was less than fully secure. Ultimately, everything went by sea. A shipment of Lunas and Il-28s left for

Cuba in early October; their nuclear warheads left even earlier, on September 15, aboard the freighter *Indigirka*, which was already scheduled to carry warheads for MRBMs and FKRs.

Khrushchev now began to wonder whether he had made a terrible mistake. The entire operation depended upon one of two things: either that the Soviets would succeed in deploying a major nuclear force undetected or that Kennedy would take the deployment in stride. Neither was beginning to look very likely. And Khrushchev had left himself with no appropriate contingency.

ON THE EVE OF CRISIS

Kennedy soon began issuing orders just in case he needed military options. On October 2, he had McNamara inform the JCS that they should be ready to launch air strikes against Cuba by October 20. Admiral Robert Dennison, commander-in-chief of American forces in the Atlantic (CINCLANT), began preparing for an invasion. Ships put to sea, aircraft redeployed, troops moved closer to Cuba.

In Cuba, the Soviets moved into high gear. Workers unloaded ships as quickly as possible. Technicians rushed to close the gaps in Cuba's air defense network. Work on the missile sites intensified. The deployment became disorderly. Weapons and equipment arrived at sites not yet ready to

---

WAS THE UNITED STATES PLANNING AN INVASION OF CUBA BEFORE THE CRISIS BROKE?

Some observers have argued that the Kennedy administration was intending to invade Cuba in the months preceding the missile crisis. Using once highly secret documents, historian James Hershberg showed that American military and civilian leaders alike spent considerable time and energy exploring military options and provocatively suggested that the administration may well have been intending an invasion.

There is no doubt the American government wanted to get rid of Fidel Castro, that it provided considerable assistance to covert operations in and against Cuba through 1962, and that one plan called for active US assistance should an uprising against Castro occur in late 1962. It is also now clear that the Pentagon began in late 1961 to develop tactics for an American invasion of Cuba and that Secretary of Defense Robert McNamara discussed these plans with the president on more than one occasion. Military preparations immediately before and during the crisis were based on these plans. However, there is no available evidence to show the administration decided at any point to attack Cuba. All of the available evidence suggests that Kennedy would have authorized military action only as a last resort. The mere existence of contingency plans is not evidence of political intentions or desires.

Figure 2.4 U-2 photograph of the first identified R-12 missile site (Courtesy John F. Kennedy Library)

receive them. Specialized vehicles and equipment moved and parked in the open. Missiles lay horizontal on open fields, covered only by missile-shaped tarpaulins. All of a sudden, things were visible from the air that ought to have been hidden.

On October 9, the US Committee on Overhead Reconnaissance (COMOR) recommended that a U-2 flight target the San Cristóbal area, west of Havana. HUMINT indicated that this was an area of particularly suspicious activity. Kennedy decided it was time to have a look and rescinded the prohibition on direct overflights. Weather delayed the mission for several days, but at 11:30 P.M. on Saturday, October 13, a U-2 piloted by Major Richard S. Heyser left Edwards Air Force Base in California. By breakfast time on Sunday it was over Cuba, and by noon it had landed in Florida with the first hard evidence of a Soviet nuclear deployment. On Monday morning, analysts at the National Photographic Interpretation Center (NPIC) outside Washington developed and analyzed the film, spotting Soviet MRBMs. McGeorge Bundy got the word late that evening. He decided not to wake the president but to let him get a good night's sleep.

It would be his last for two weeks.

CHAPTER 3

From Discovery to Blockade

KENNEDY WAS READING the newspaper on Tuesday morning, October 16, when McGeorge Bundy interrupted with the news that a U-2 had photographed nuclear missiles in Cuba. The president was not easily rattled, but Bundy could see a wave of disbelief, shock, anger, and fear wash over him in the brief moment it took him to react. Kennedy knew he was about to face the most difficult challenge of his presidency.

The president felt at once that Khrushchev had ignored his warnings and deliberately misled him. Khrushchev was attempting through deception to present Kennedy with a fait accompli. Both in his public statements and through an active back-channel between Bobby Kennedy and a Soviet intelligence officer in Washington named Georgi Bolshakov, Khrushchev had insisted that the Soviet Union was deploying only "defensive" weapons to Cuba. Through Bolshakov, Khrushchev had also promised not to do anything to rock the boat before the mid-term elections in November. Kennedy took the deception very personally. As he reportedly told his brother: "He can't do this to *me!*"

The president immediately asked Bundy to assemble a select group to advise him on an American response. This group would eventually become known as the "ExComm," or the Executive Committee of the National Security Council.[1] Meeting almost every day and sometimes more than once

---

1. J. F. K. signed National Security Action Memorandum (NSAM) 196, which formally established the ExComm, on October 22. Its regular members included the president as chair, Vice President Lyndon Johnson, Secretary of State Dean Rusk, Secretary of Defense Robert McNamara, Secretary of the Treasury C. Douglas Dillon, Attorney General Robert Kennedy, DCI John McCone, Undersecretary of State U. Alexis Johnson, Deputy Secretary of Defense Roswell Gilpatric, Chairman of the JCS General Maxwell Taylor, Ambassador-at-Large Llewellyn Thompson, Special Counsel Theodore Sorensen, and Special Assistant to the President for National Security Affairs McGeorge Bundy. Various others attended at the president's request from time to time, and some of the regular members missed particular meetings so that the roster of those present changed frequently. Also present at the first meeting, for example, were Charles Bohlen, an old Soviet hand who had recently been appointed ambassador to France; Assistant Secretary

WERE THE SOVIET WEAPONS "OFFENSIVE" OR "DEFENSIVE"?

Both in his public warnings in September and through back-channel communications, President Kennedy consistently said that he would not tolerate "offensive" Soviet weapons in Cuba. Khrushchev consistently insisted that he was sending only "defensive" weapons. Was Khrushchev lying?

Technically, no. There are two different ways of distinguishing "offensive" from "defensive" weapons. The first is by capability: if a weapon is useful in an attack against another's territory, it is offensive, while if it is useful only in thwarting an attack against oneself, it is defensive. A long-range bomber would be an offensive weapon in this view, and a land mine would be a defensive weapon. The strategic missiles and Il-28s Khrushchev was sending to Cuba were clearly capable of striking the United States and, therefore, "offensive" according to this understanding. But another way of drawing the distinction is by intention: in this view, if a weapon is meant to be used for aggression or conquest, it is offensive, while if it is meant only for deterrence or only for self-protection, it is defensive. Since Khrushchev saw these weapons primarily as deterrents and did not imagine using them to start a war, they were, in this understanding, defensive. (A third, rather crude way of drawing the distinction, is simply to say: "My weapons are defensive; yours are offensive." To some extent, both Kennedy and Khrushchev may have seen matters in this light as well!)

Despite the fact that Khrushchev saw these weapons as defensive (since he drew the distinction in his own mind according to intention rather than capability), there is little doubt that he knew what kinds of weapons Kennedy sought to keep out of Cuba. By insisting that he was sending only defensive weapons, Khrushchev was splitting hairs. So while he may not technically have been lying, he was certainly deliberately misleading Kennedy on the true nature of the deployment so that he could present him later with a fait accompli.

a day, the ExComm played a very important role in the crisis, though its role varied somewhat as time when on. Early in the crisis, Kennedy used the ExComm as a source of ideas and viewpoints; later in the crisis, he used it more as a vehicle for legitimating his own decisions. His reliance on the ExComm, in other words, decreased over time as he became more confident in the wisdom of his own judgment.

Kennedy wished to keep the ExComm's deliberations quiet so that neither journalists nor Soviet spies would catch wind of the fact that the United

---

of Defense Paul Nitze; Undersecretary of State George Ball; Assistant Secretary of State for Inter–American Affairs Edwin Martin; Deputy Director of Central Intelligence Marshall "Pat" Carter; and the director of NPIC, Arthur Lundahl. Absent were Alexis Johnson and John McCone.

Figure 3.1   The Executive Committee of the National Security Council (ExComm) (Courtesy John F. Kennedy Library)

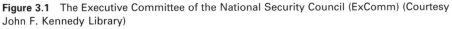

States had discovered missiles in Cuba before Kennedy had decided upon a response. As a result, members of the ExComm took extreme precautions coming and going, sometimes using underground tunnels rather than risking being seen arriving in groups at the White House in chauffeured automobiles. Even their own families had no inkling of what they were doing or why they were working such long hours.

Unbeknownst to all but his brother, the president had decided in the summer to install secret tape-recording equipment in the Oval Office and Cabinet Room—presumably so that he would have an accurate record on the basis of which to write his memoirs—so, fortunately for historians, many of the ExComm's candid deliberations are now available verbatim. In the tapes and transcripts of these meetings, we see a group of earnest, thoughtful, but generally baffled men groping their way—sometimes together, often not— toward a solution to a problem all had feared but few had imagined they would ever have to confront.

THE STORM BEFORE THE CALM

The atmosphere on day one was tense. The first item of business was the U-2 photos. It was the job of NPIC director Arthur Lundahl to show the assembled men the pictures and to explain what they revealed: a handful of tarpaulins covering R-12 MRBMs strewn about an open field at a half-finished missile site west of Havana. What the CIA did not know was how many other missiles might be present in Cuba and whether any were ready to fire. Nor did anyone know exactly what Khrushchev was up to. These were crucial pieces of information: without them, it was impossible to diagnose the problem and identify a solution. If there were more missiles in Cuba as yet undiscovered and if they were, in fact, already operational (eight were, unbeknownst to the ExComm), then it would be impossible to have high confidence that the United States could destroy Soviet strategic nuclear capability in Cuba in a swift surprise strike and highly risky to try. If Khrushchev had intended the deployment (for example) to give him leverage on Berlin, then the crisis would likely spill over into Europe. Diplomacy might work if the deployment had been motivated by a sense of need or fear, but it would probably backfire if the deployment had been an opportunistic challenge. The only thing that was crystal clear on that very first day of deliberation was that everyone but McCone had been horribly, horribly wrong about what Khrushchev might actually do. This was something about which the president could not afford to be wrong again.

The situation had one saving grace: Kennedy could afford to take some time to decide how to respond. No one else knew that the United States had discovered missiles in Cuba. He needed more information, and he had the luxury of being able to wait for it. This was crucial because he was angry and belligerent and, if forced to respond right away, he almost certainly would have opted for military action of some kind—either a surgical air strike to knock out the known missile sites, a broader air strike that would also include Cuba's airfields and SAMs, or a massive invasion that would have as its goal ridding Cuba not only of Soviet military hardware but of Castro as well.

Kennedy's belligerence was, in a sense, perfectly understandable. News of the discovery had been a terrible blow. He felt deceived, insulted, challenged. His emotion running high, it was natural for him to want to lash out. The only nonviolent option Kennedy entertained on the morning of October 16 was a blockade, which he felt would be too easy for the Soviets to circumvent ("I don't see how we could prevent further [missiles] from coming in by submarine," he said, more than once, betraying a surprising lack of awareness for an old navy man that submarines have neither hatches nor holds large enough for strategic nuclear missiles). But military action was very risky. Chairman of the JCS General Maxwell Taylor candidly stated that an air strike would "never be 100 percent" effective. McNamara insisted that it was too dangerous to attempt an air strike after any of the missiles had become operational, as some might already be. Bobby Kennedy wondered where and how Khrushchev might retaliate. Initially, none of these concerns put the president off. "At least we're going to do number one [the surgical air strike]," Kennedy said toward the end of the first meeting, "so it seems to me that we don't have to wait very long. We ought to be making those preparations." This prompted Bundy rather nervously to wonder "whether we have definitely decided against a political track," adding "I, myself, think we ought to work out a contingency on that."

Kennedy asked the group to reconvene at six o'clock. Taylor met with the other chiefs in the meantime and returned to report a consensus that a surgical strike would not be enough. What was needed, at a minimum, was a massive air strike against the full set of military targets in Cuba. But there was still no consensus among the group as a whole. Bobby Kennedy argued now for engineering an excuse to invade ("sink the *Maine* again or something"). McNamara pushed for a blockade. Bundy began to lean slightly in the direction of air strikes. The president—still belligerent—felt instinctively that he had to meet Khrushchev's challenge with force.

These early deliberations are striking in two crucial respects. First, the ExComm did not reach closure on the nature of the Soviet threat. Some, such as Taylor, thought that the deployment drastically altered the global balance of power; others, such as McNamara, felt that it did not since the United States was already vulnerable to nuclear fire from Soviet submarines or weapons based in the USSR. Kennedy, quite clearly, saw the missiles primarily as a political threat rather than a military one. Second, while it is true that the ExComm examined a variety of options, they did not proceed methodically through them, nor did they spend equal time on them all. One option—"do nothing"—was more or less ruled out at the beginning. Purely diplomatic approaches—public or private, bilateral or multilateral—received very little attention at all. To the extent that the group considered diplomacy as a response, they did so generally as an adjunct to, or preparation for, military action.

It was fortunate for the ExComm that the options being considered did not, in fact, come out of thin air. This accelerated the process of evaluating their strengths and weaknesses. Some had been bandied about publicly for months. As we discussed in the previous chapter, prominent Republicans had been advocating blockade or invasion and Kennedy himself had asked the military to work up various contingencies. Public opinion polls taken prior to October 1962, however, showed that two-thirds of Americans opposed the use of US troops to overthrow Castro; but that was before the discovery of missiles.

On Wednesday, October 17, the president decided to keep his normal schedule, so as not to arouse suspicions. The ExComm met without him, and in the free-for-all discussion, it became apparent that there was no progress toward consensus. If anything, the group's views began to diverge even more widely as new voices made themselves heard. McCone, now back in Washington, argued against a sudden air strike, which, he felt, would put the United States in a difficult moral position—a kind of Pearl Harbor in reverse. McCone's view was that Khrushchev should have twenty-four hours to agree to withdraw all strategic nuclear missiles and any dual-use weapons systems capable of inflicting damage upon the United States—for example,

---

WHAT ROLE DID MORAL CONSIDERATIONS PLAY IN THE ExCOMM'S DELIBERATIONS?

McCone's qualms against a surprise air attack are a striking example of an important official taking moral considerations seriously. In part, McCone's sensitivities to moral considerations flowed from his religious convictions. A devout Catholic, McCone had earlier opposed attempts to assassinate Castro, fearing, among other things, that by supporting them he might risk excommunication.

Others on the ExComm also felt queasy about a surprise attack for moral reasons. George Ball was the first to raise the parallel in an ExComm meeting, on October 18 ("A course of action where we strike without warning is like Pearl Harbor. It's the kind of conduct that one might expect of the Soviet Union. It is not conduct that one expects of the United States.") Dean Rusk was persuaded, as was Bobby Kennedy, who wrongly claimed credit in his memoir for raising the issue.

There was no consensus, however, on the question of whether the Pearl Harbor analogy was appropriate. Paul Nitze thought it was "nonsense." Dean Acheson agreed. In their view, the provocation and deception of the Soviet deployment fully justified whatever action was necessary to deal with it. Their dissenting views did not necessarily mean that they were insensitive to moral considerations in policy deliberations; they merely thought that these particular qualms were misplaced.

The president, of course, ultimately opted against a surprise attack, in large part because of the risks of escalation it would entail. Behind his caution was a genuine moral horror of the prospect of nuclear war. But neither the president nor any of his advisers thought in terms of moral absolutes. Moral considerations weighed in the balance alongside practical and political ones. In this respect, the Kennedy administration was typical of political leadership groups—indeed, of people in general.

MiG-21 fighters and Il-28 bombers—and only *then*, if he failed to comply with the ultimatum, should the United States attack. Former Secretary of State Dean Acheson was less skittish, favoring a surgical air strike to destroy the known missiles quickly. Former president Dwight D. Eisenhower, whom Kennedy asked McCone to consult that day, argued for air strikes against the full set of military targets in Cuba. But pushing now in the opposite direction were Charles Bohlen and UN Ambassador Adlai Stevenson, who argued for a purely diplomatic approach. Stevenson went so far as to suggest, in a memorandum that annoyed the president, that the United States consider trading Jupiter missiles in Turkey for Soviet missiles in Cuba, an option the president would ultimately embrace.

With the president's advisers even further from consensus on what to do, Bobby Kennedy received a "personal message" from Khrushchev via his back-channel contact, Georgi Bolshakov: "Under no circumstances would surface-to-surface missiles be sent to Cuba."

NARROWING THE OPTIONS

By Thursday, October 18, the CIA had found yet more missile sites, providing the ExComm with new U-2 photos revealing construction of a launch site for the R-14, a more advanced, longer-range missile. Within days, photoreconnaissance would identify two more R-14 bases. Once these missiles became operational, more than 90 percent of the American population would be vulnerable to a nuclear strike from Cuba, as would the backbone of the American strategic deterrent—the airfields and missile silos dotting the US Midwest.

The discovery of IRBM sites dramatically increased the scope of any air strike option. The chiefs decided that limited air strikes were no longer feasible; at a minimum, the United States should conduct strikes against the full set of military targets in Cuba, and a follow-on invasion would be a practical necessity. But the military response all by itself began to look less and less appealing to many others. As the scope of the military option increased, so also did the political costs. And then there was the question of warheads. Were any in Cuba? If so, for which missiles, how many, and where? American intelligence had found no hard evidence of nuclear warheads in Cuba and, indeed, never confirmed that they were present during the crisis

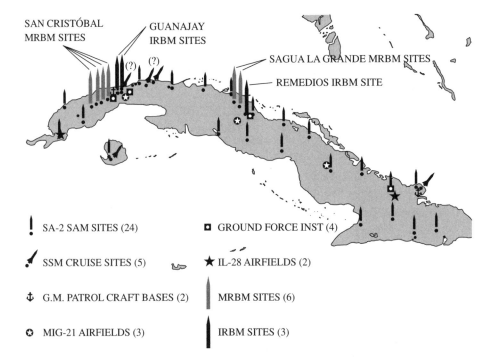

Figure 3.2 Soviet forces in Cuba (as identified by US intelligence, October 1962)

itself. In fact, many were, as most American officials were inclined to assume, fortuitously preferring to err on the side of caution.[2]

During the ExComm meeting on October 18, the options finally began to narrow to two: blockade or air strike. In fact, these two options were not as dichotomous as they might seem, and they did not necessarily preclude other possibilities. Most around the table understood that an air strike would almost certainly be followed by an invasion; those who favored military action understood that a blockade would be imposed as a matter of course while military operations were under way. So the real choice was between a blockade alone, holding further military options in reserve while Khrushchev had a chance to agree to back down, or an attack without warning.

Llewellyn Thompson, one of the Kennedy administration's top Soviet experts, joined the group for the discussion on October 18 and immediately championed the blockade option. In Thompson's view, Khrushchev had deployed missiles to Cuba for the purpose of dealing them away, most likely for concessions on Berlin. In this he was mistaken, but his conviction that he was right led him to stress the importance of giving Khrushchev an opportunity to negotiate. A sudden military strike would, in effect, force Khrushchev to retaliate, setting in train a sequence of actions and reactions that would be difficult to anticipate and control. Thompson was confident that Khrushchev would not attempt to run the blockade, but worried that it would not actually force cessation of work on the missile sites in Cuba. Those who leaned toward the blockade therefore tended to favor giving Khrushchev limited time to comply with American demands to withdraw. The group spent a good deal of time considering the various prices Khrushchev might demand in return for agreeing to withdraw missiles from Cuba, very quickly identifying as one possible quid pro quo American Jupiter missiles in Turkey.

One of the difficulties with a blockade was that it was technically an act of war. Some were not much concerned by this, but Kennedy eventually came to worry about the optics of declaring war on Cuba or the Soviet Union, either explicitly or implicitly. The concern to find a way of justifying a blockade legally (Thompson rightly noted the curious weight the Soviets placed on matters of legality) without technically entering a state of war prompted a good deal of creative discussion. Rusk and Martin suggested securing authorization under the Rio treaty from the OAS, and later that night the State Department's deputy legal adviser, Leonard Meeker, ingeniously suggested calling it a "quarantine."

Kennedy was now eager to come to a decision. He was still unsure about what he would do, but he did not want things to drag out much longer. He

---

2. A retrospective postmortem of US intelligence identified nuclear-warhead transport vans and concluded that nuclear warheads probably were present during the crisis.

was particularly keen that everything would be ready for whichever option he chose. Sensing the president's desire to reach closure, McNamara suggested forming two groups to work up the two emerging options so that Kennedy had a clear basis on which to decide. Kennedy pressed Taylor to be ready for military action as soon as possible in case he chose the air strike option, by Saturday if possible. Taylor wanted more time—until Tuesday, preferably— since existing plans had to be updated in light of the new intelligence about IRBMs. But Kennedy urged him to get things ready as quickly as he could.

At five o'clock, Kennedy and Rusk left to keep a previously scheduled meeting with Soviet Foreign Minister Andrei Gromyko. The meeting took place in the Oval Office and was surely one of the more curious—and certainly one of the most strained—Cold War encounters. Kennedy kept from Gromyko the fact that he was aware of missiles in Cuba. The president went so far as to read from his September statements, but Gromyko never suspected that Kennedy knew and never volunteered any information. He merely repeated the standard Soviet line about sending only defensive weapons to Cuba. In his report to Moscow shortly after the meeting, Gromyko confidently assured his colleagues that the situation in Washington was "wholly satisfactory."

Figure 3.3 Soviet Foreign Minister Gromyko visits the White House, October 18, 1962 (Courtesy John F. Kennedy Library)

Gromyko was very relieved that Kennedy did not ask him directly if the USSR had missiles in Cuba, for this meant he neither had to lie nor had to tell the truth. He could, as he always preferred, simply remain silent. "It is better to commit one thousand sins of omission," Gromyko was famous for telling Soviet diplomats, "than one sin of commission."

While Kennedy and Gromyko played out their charade, the ExComm continued to meet. Opinion now swung clearly toward the blockade as an initial step. Its crucial advantage—that it was less likely to trigger an extreme reaction from Khrushchev—began to loom larger in people's minds. Indeed, this began looming larger in Kennedy's mind as well. As his anger cooled, he began to focus more on the importance of avoiding irrevocable steps down the road to war. Kennedy was primed to worry about this. He had recently read Barbara Tuchman's new book *The Guns of August*, which detailed how European leaders stumbled unwittingly into World War I through a combination of ignorance, misjudgment, denial, headstrong false confidence, and irrevocable acts. The blockade, at least, did not require the United States to fire the first shot. But neither did it preclude the possibility of military action later, if military action were required.

But what seemed like an emergent consensus quickly began to unravel after the president met with the group once again. There were lingering doubts about the effectiveness of a blockade. The president sent the group back to reconsider their differences. He was scheduled to make campaign appearances in Cleveland and Chicago the next day, and he decided to go ahead with the trip since he was not yet in a position to commit to a course of action anyway. Nothing would happen for at least a couple of days, and he did not want to risk arousing suspicions by canceling. But before going, he wanted to take the chiefs' pulse, and he wanted to brief Bobby, who would quarterback the ExComm in his absence. He found the chiefs eager to mount the large air strike but divided on the utility of invasion. They vigorously opposed a small-scale surgical strike on the missile sites alone. As the commandant of the Marine Corps, David Shoup, told his fellow chiefs of staff (as captured on the White House tape recorders) following their Friday morning meeting with the president: "you can't f— around and go take a missile out. . . . You can't fiddle around with the SAM sites. You go in and take out the goddamn thing that's going to stop you from doing your job."

DECISION: THE CALM BEFORE THE STORM

The president's assignment for his brother was to bring the ExComm to consensus and to call him when he did. The ExComm now split into two groups, whose job was to make the strongest possible case for either the blockade or the air strike option. Acheson, Bundy, Dillon, R. F. K., and McCone worked up the air strike; Ball, Alexis Johnson, McNamara, Rusk, and

Thompson worked up the blockade. During the course of the day on Friday, Bobby actually came to favor the blockade as the initial step, and the blockade option came out on top. Bobby called his brother and told him to return to Washington. The president, in turn, told his press secretary, Pierre Salinger, to announce that he was cutting short his campaign trip because of a "slight cold." After dutifully telling the press, Salinger joined Kennedy in the back of the presidential plane. "What's going on?" Salinger asked. "When you find out," Kennedy replied, "you'll grab your balls."

Back in Washington on the morning of Saturday, October 20, the president learned that the CIA considered that as many as eight of the R-12s in Cuba could now be launched within eight hours. The prospect of nuclear retaliation against cities in the eastern United States took the wind out of any remaining enthusiasm Kennedy had for the air strike option.

A majority of Kennedy's advisers, meeting on Saturday morning officially as the entire National Security Council, had converged around the blockade option. But the question remained of what to do if the Soviets did not agree to dismantle the existing missile sites. On this, there was disagreement. Many favored following up with an air strike if Khrushchev did not agree to withdraw the missiles within forty-eight or seventy-two hours. McNamara argued against an ultimatum and stressed the importance of being willing to negotiate. It was McNamara, not Adlai Stevenson, who raised the possibility of withdrawing US missiles from Turkey and Italy and possibly limiting the period of time in which the United States would remain at Guantánamo. Stevenson forcefully echoed McNamara's view, insisting that the United States try to avoid a military conflict by offering to remove its missiles from Turkey and evacuate Guantánamo, a position for which the Kennedy administration later hung him out to dry by leaking to journalists Charles Bartlett and Stewart Alsop, who duly ran with the story in the *Saturday Evening Post*, that "Adlai wanted a Munich." Kennedy rejected any linkage to Guantánamo and refused to open with an offer of a missile trade, but he instructed Nitze to look into the feasibility of withdrawing missiles from Turkey and Italy.

Blockade it would be—at least as an opening move. The focus of discussion therefore shifted to mechanics and packaging. Initially, the president decided that the blockade would include only offensive military hardware; petroleum, oil, and lubricants (POL) could be added at a later date if necessary. Officially, the blockade would be labeled a "quarantine," and the White House would seek legal cover by securing authorization from the OAS. The legal justification would not persuade everyone, so to deflect attention from the issue, Kennedy would stress the deception and duplicity of the Soviet deployment in his speech announcing the discovery of the missiles and the imposition of the quarantine.

On Sunday, October 21, Kennedy met with the commander of the US Air Force (USAF) Tactical Air Command, General Walter Sweeney, to reexamine the air strike option one last time. Sweeney told him frankly there could be

WAS THE "QUARANTINE" LEGAL?

Compared to the domestic law of a modern, sophisticated country, international law is patchy, underdeveloped, and vague. It therefore leaves open a great deal of room for debate on many important questions, and the legality of the "quarantine" was certainly one.

Most international law is contained in duly ratified treaties and agreements and in the "customary practices of civilized nations." In important respects, the master international legal document is the charter of the UN. Typically, deciding whether something is legal under international law involves weighing considerations for and against and deciding who has the better argument on balance. Courts and tribunals sometimes perform this function, but in the Cuban missile crisis, as in many other cases, the real trial takes place in the court of world opinion.

The best argument against the legality of the quarantine was that the Soviet Union had a presumptive right to freedom of navigation on the high seas and that the Soviet Union and Cuba, as sovereign states, had a right to cooperate militarily as they saw fit. The Kennedy administration could not argue against these claims but could try to argue that, in this particular case, other considerations trumped them. The best way to make that case, Kennedy's legal advisers felt, was to focus on the threat to the security of the hemisphere that a Soviet deployment of nuclear missiles represented. Article 51 of the UN charter recognizes the individual and collective right of states to self-defense, and Article 52 authorizes regional security arrangements. The charter of the OAS and the Inter-American Treaty of Reciprocal Assistance (the Rio Treaty), invoking the UN charter, gave the United States legal hooks on which to hang its case.

Was the American case for the legality of the quarantine weightier than the Soviet case against it? Opinions differed at the time. But by focusing in its diplomacy on the deception surrounding the Soviet deployment, the United States was able to demonize Khrushchev in the eyes of much of the world, which inclined the court of public opinion to give the United States the benefit of the doubt.

no guarantee that an attack would destroy all the missiles in Cuba. Some missiles would likely survive. Kennedy now realized that neither a blockade nor an air strike could be relied upon to solve the problem of missiles already in Cuba. "It looked like we would have all the difficulties of Pearl Harbor," he told his staff, "and not have finished the job." Nevertheless, he ordered the air force to be prepared to carry out air strikes any time after Monday morning.

The president also met that day with David Ormsby-Gore, the British ambassador to Washington and an old Kennedy family friend. Ormsby-Gore had already learned through intelligence channels on Friday that a crisis over Cuba was imminent and had so advised British Prime Minister Harold

Macmillan. To Ormsby-Gore, Kennedy confessed almost admiringly that Khrushchev had pinned him on the horns of a dilemma. On the one hand, if the United States acted with violence, Khrushchev had an excuse to go into Berlin; on the other hand, if it did not, the United States would look weak to its friends and allies. Kennedy asked for his old friend's view. The ambassador strongly supported a blockade. He also told Kennedy that "an invasion without internal popular support usually led to endless trouble. The idea of a puppet regime kept in power by American marines was not a happy prospect."

Kennedy sent a personal letter to Macmillan as well. While the American ambassador in London would brief the prime minister more fully on Monday, Kennedy explained he wanted Macmillan "to have this message tonight, so that you may have as much time as possible to consider the dangers we will now have to face together." The president acknowledged he was informing rather than consulting the British at this stage, noting somewhat apologetically that he had found it "absolutely essential in the interests of security and speed to make my first decision on my own responsibility." From that point on, however, he and Macmillan would "have to act most closely together." Immediately after his televised broadcast the following day, the president telephoned Macmillan, the first of many such calls during the crisis.

As more officials became involved in preparations for the president's speech and for the blockade, word of the crisis finally began to leak to the press. The president spoke personally to editors of several newspapers, asking them to hold their stories until after his speech. One newspaper actually first learned details of the matter from the president's call. The first press reports the following day referred only to the forthcoming speech and to a serious looming crisis.

Monday morning was a day of tying off loose ends before the crisis broke. This included briefing other important allies. Kennedy sent Dean Acheson to Paris to brief French President Charles de Gaulle and to present the American case to NATO. Other emissaries briefed not only Prime Minister Macmillan but also Canadian Prime Minister John Diefenbaker and West German Chancellor Konrad Adenauer. Personal messages from the president went to Mayor Willy Brandt of West Berlin, Premier Amintore Fanfani of Italy, and Prime Minister Jawaharlal Nehru of India. The Department of State sent presidential letters to the various governments of Latin America, along with notices of the OAS meeting called by the United States for Tuesday. Similar letters also went to countries then sitting on the UN Security Council.

Just before Kennedy went on television, he met with a group of congressional leaders to brief them on the situation and his impending announcement. Many were unimpressed with the blockade decision and called for stronger military action. The president argued that the situation was very tense, and he emphasized the dangers of military escalation. "If we go into Cuba," he said, "we have to all realize that we have taken the chance that these missiles, which are ready to fire, won't be fired." Though he was prepared to take that chance, it was, he said, "one hell of a gamble."

CHAPTER 4

The Perfect Storm

As President Kennedy and his advisers deliberated during the "private week" of the crisis, an atmosphere of calm satisfaction pervaded Moscow. Khrushchev, following the progress of Anadyr closely, saw no signs of trouble on the horizon. Soviet intelligence had noticed an increase in US military activity in the Caribbean, but this was hardly surprising in view of the increased volume of Soviet shipping. The main thing was that Washington was silent. Gromyko's visit to the White House had been the perfect opportunity for Kennedy to speak if he had something new to say, and he had not. Either Kennedy knew nothing about the missiles, some of which were now becoming operational, or he had discovered them and seemed to be taking them in stride. Either possibility suited Khrushchev just fine.

Algerian president Ahmed Ben Bella was Castro's guest at dinner on October 17, having flown directly to Havana from Washington. There, Kennedy had told him point-blank that the United States had no intention of intervening in Cuba, although the president added the customary proviso that if the Soviets were to turn Cuba into an "offensive" military base, the United States would keep its options open. Castro seemed calm, almost dismissive of the American threat. The Cuban leadership had also decided, it seems, that the Soviet deployment either would go unnoticed or would deter an American attack. Raúl Castro had confidently told Alekseev in September that the danger of American intervention had passed. The *Dirección General de Inteligencia* (DGI), Cuba's intelligence service, was not so sure. At roughly the same time Castro was hosting Ben Bella, the DGI warned that the United States would strike suddenly and massively once the full nature and magnitude of the Soviet deployment became clear and urged that the armed forces and the Ministry of the Interior move to full alert.

Everything changed on October 22. The GRU (*Glavnoye Razvedyvatelnoye Upravlenie*) began reporting highly unusual US military activity. The KGB caught wind that something big was happening in Washington. Word reached the Kremlin that Kennedy had requested airtime for a speech that evening, and rumors were that the topic would be either Cuba or Berlin.

In a sudden sense of crisis, Khrushchev called an emergency meeting of the Presidium.

There was, according to the Soviet record of the meeting, a sense of doom hanging in the air. Khrushchev, who was convinced Kennedy would announce the discovery of missiles in Cuba, launched into a lament: he had come so close, he should have done things differently, he should have published the treaty. Malinovsky tried to reassure the assembled group that the United States would not act immediately; they would need at least twenty-four hours even if they were preparing an airborne assault. The Soviets had time to respond. But Khrushchev was pessimistic. "This may end in a big war."

Khrushchev and his colleagues did not know what Kennedy planned to say or what action he would announce, but it is interesting to note that they considered, if briefly, the very same broad set of options that the ExComm had been wrestling with for a week. Khrushchev even speculated that Kennedy might announce a blockade and do nothing. But everyone in the room thought it unlikely. What was likely, they felt, was a war in the Caribbean within hours or, at most, a few days.

If an attack were imminent, Pliyev needed instructions. A debate ensued about what to tell him. It was important, the Presidium felt, to reduce as far as possible the danger of unintended nuclear war. They agreed that while Pliyev should put his forces on full alert, he should be told that under no circumstances should he use nuclear weapons without explicit authorization from Moscow. But the more they thought about it, the more they realized that Pliyev's defense would be hopeless if he were denied the use of tactical nuclear weapons. So they wrote out a second set of instructions—the same terms agreed to in September, which Malinovsky had at that time refused to sign—categorically forbidding the use of strategic nuclear weapons without authorization from Moscow but permitting Pliyev to use tactical nuclear weapons against invading American forces if communications with Moscow were cut. Malinovsky suggested, and the Presidium agreed, that they transmit the first, more restrictive set of instructions right away but hold the second set of instructions in reserve, awaiting developments. Malinovsky did not want to provoke or give justification for an American preemptive strike by predelegating authority to use nuclear weapons via a message that American intelligence might intercept.

THE SPEECH

At 7:00 P.M., President Kennedy went on radio and television to give the most ominous presidential speech of the Cold War. "This government, as promised, has maintained the closest surveillance of the Soviet military buildup on the island of Cuba," he began:

The purpose of these bases can be none other than to provide a nuclear strike capability against the Western Hemisphere. . . .

This action also contradicts the repeated assurances of Soviet spokesmen, both publicly and privately delivered, that the arms buildup in Cuba would retain its original defensive character and that the Soviet Union had no need or desire to station strategic missiles on the territory of any other nation. . . .

Neither the United States of America nor the world community of nations can tolerate deliberate deception and offensive threats on the part of any nation, large or small. . . .

Acting, therefore, in the defense of our own security and of the entire Western Hemisphere, and under the authority entrusted to me by the Constitution as endorsed by the resolution of the Congress, I have directed that the following initial steps be taken immediately:

First: To halt this offensive buildup, a strict quarantine on all offensive military equipment under shipment to Cuba is being initiated. All ships of any kind bound for Cuba from whatever nation or port will, if found to contain cargoes of offensive weapons, be turned back. . . .

Second: I have directed the continued and increased close surveillance of Cuba and its military buildup. . . . Should these offensive military preparations continue, thus increasing the threat to the hemisphere, further action will be justified. I have directed the Armed Forces to prepare for any eventualities. . . .

Third: It shall be the policy of this Nation to regard any nuclear missile launched from Cuba against any nation in the Western Hemisphere as an attack by the Soviet Union on the United States, requiring a full retaliatory response upon the Soviet Union.

Fourth: As a necessary military precaution, I have reinforced our base at Guantánamo, evacuated today the dependents of our personnel there, and ordered additional military units to be on a standby alert basis.

Fifth: We are calling tonight for an immediate meeting of the . . . Organization of American States, to consider this threat to hemispheric security and to invoke articles 6 and 8 of the Rio Treaty in support of all necessary action. The United Nations Charter allows for regional security arrangements—and the nations of this hemisphere decided long ago against the military presence of outside powers. Our other allies around the world have also been alerted.

Sixth: Under the Charter of the United Nations, we are asking tonight that an emergency meeting of the Security Council be convoked without delay to take action against this latest Soviet threat to world peace. Our resolution will call for the prompt dismantling and withdrawal of all offensive weapons in Cuba, under the supervision of U.N. observers, before the quarantine can be lifted.

Seventh and finally: I call upon Chairman Khrushchev to halt and eliminate this clandestine, reckless and provocative threat to world peace and to stable relations between our two nations. I call upon him further to abandon this course of world domination, and to join in an historic effort to end the perilous arms race and to transform the history of man. . . .

My fellow citizens, let no one doubt that this is a difficult and dangerous effort on which we have set out. No one can foresee precisely what course it will take or what costs or casualties will be incurred. Many months of sacrifice and self-discipline lie ahead—months in which both our patience and our will will be tested, months in which many threats and denunciations will keep us aware of our dangers. But the greatest danger of all would be to do nothing.

The path we have chosen for the present is full of hazards, as all paths are; but it is the one most consistent with our character and courage as a nation and our commitments around the world. The cost of freedom is always high—but Americans have always paid it. And one path we shall never choose, and that is the path of surrender or submission.

As the president was speaking—very early in the morning of October 23, Moscow time—the American embassy delivered a copy of his speech to the Kremlin. If the general reaction to his speech in the United States and other Western countries was apprehensive, the reaction of Soviet leaders was a mixture of outrage and relief. Khrushchev saw that he had some breathing space. He decided to continue with construction of the missile sites. The Presidium ordered a precautionary, low-level alert of some Soviet and Warsaw Pact military forces. The Kremlin recognized that the American navy posed a danger to Soviet ships en route to Cuba and issued instructions to some ships that had recently left for Cuba or were just leaving to return to port. But the *Aleksandrovsk*, with its precious cargo of warheads, was ordered to make for the closest Cuban port with all possible speed. Four freighters carrying the full complement of 24 R-14 missiles also continued on.

Khrushchev sent two personal messages on Tuesday. One was to President Kennedy, the first of almost a dozen he sent during the crisis. Khrushchev decried the blockade and warned Soviet ships would not respect it. He insisted the weapons in Cuba were defensive in nature and described American actions as outright banditry. He did not tell the American president that certain Soviet ships had been ordered to turn back. The second message, to Fidel Castro, assured the Cuban leader that the Soviet Union would not back down. But Khrushchev also neglected to tell Castro that he had ordered some ships back to port. Belying his apparent calm, the Soviet premier spent that night on a couch in his office, fully clothed and awaiting possible "alarming news." Castro ordered Cuban forces to their highest level of alert, sent his brother Raúl to direct defensive preparations in eastern Cuba, and sent Che Guevara to direct preparations in the western

MRBM LAUNCH SITE 1
SAN CRISTOBAL, CUBA
23 OCTOBER 1962

MISSILE ERECTOR   CABLE

MISSILE SHELTER TENT

TRACKED PRIME MOVERS

FUEL TANK TRAILERS

OXIDIZER TANK TRAILERS

Figure 4.1 Low-level reconnaissance photograph of San Cristóbal R-12 missile site (Courtesy John F. Kennedy Library)

provinces. Over the course of three days, more than 300,000 Cubans took up arms and prepared for the worst.

Coincident with the president's speech, the Pentagon ordered the US military to Defence Condition 3 (DEFCON 3), the level of alert halfway between the normal peacetime DEFCON 5 and the maximum possible DEFCON 1. Interceptor aircraft were dispersed and, for the first time, armed with nuclear weapons. Even before the president's speech, the Strategic Air Command (SAC) went to a higher level of preparedness: one in every eight strategic bombers was to be airborne at all times, to ensure that some survived in the event of a Soviet surprise attack. The president ordered military preparations in Germany in case the Soviet Union attempted a retaliatory blockade of Berlin. Worried as well about an accidental nuclear war, he also gave special instructions to prevent the firing of a Jupiter missile from Italy or Turkey (at this time, American nuclear missiles did not have electronic controls to prevent unauthorized launches).

The Pentagon also ordered the American officer who served as the Supreme Allied Commander in Europe (SACEUR), General Lauris Norstad, to request NATO allies to place their forces on high alert as well. But Norstad opted only to take limited measures. The allies were uneasy. While publicly supporting the president, many allied governments were alarmed by America's apparent fixation with Castro and the danger of Cuba diverting attention from the critical issue of Berlin. They worried, too, that Kennedy might be prone to overreaction. Even as staunch a Kennedy friend as Harold Macmillan commented privately that Europe had for years been within range of Soviet nuclear missiles. Diefenbaker, whose personal relationship with Kennedy was very rocky, worried about provoking the Soviet Union and initially refused to order the Canadian armed forces to go to higher alert. They did so anyway.[1]

CARROTS AND STICKS

At the request of the United States, the OAS met in Washington on Tuesday morning, October 23. By a vote of 20–0, with three abstentions, the OAS approved a resolution endorsing not only the quarantine but further unspecified actions necessary to ensure that the missiles in Cuba would not threaten the Western Hemisphere. The UN Security Council also met in special session on Tuesday afternoon. US Ambassador Adlai Stevenson denounced the Soviet deployment and characterized Cuba as "an accomplice in the communist enterprise of world domination." Acting without instructions from Moscow and totally in the dark about the deployment, Soviet ambassador Valerian Zorin denied that there were missiles in Cuba and categorically refused to answer further questions.

Zorin was not the only Soviet official forced to wing it. Neither Georgi Bolshakov, the Kennedys' back-channel contact to Khrushchev, nor even Anatoly Dobrynin, the ambassador to the United States, had been informed of the deployment. (Nearly thirty years later, at a conference in Moscow, when Dobrynin complained about being kept in the dark, Gromyko turned to him and said: "I didn't tell you about the missiles? Oh . . . it must have been a very big secret!") Caught off guard, Soviet officials scrambled for information but in the meantime had to make do as best they could. Occasionally, they stumbled. Zorin genuinely believed on Tuesday that there were no missiles in Cuba, but his earnest denials backfired two days later when Stevenson, in a dramatic move designed to dispel all skepticism, showed a spellbound session of the Security Council and a global television audience

---

1. Diefenbaker's minister of defense ordered a heightened alert on his own authority. The close operational integration of the US and Canadian armed forces meant that a heightened level of preparedness was, in certain respects, almost unavoidable.

Figure 4.2   Kennedy signs the quarantine proclamation (Courtesy John F. Kennedy Library)

enlargements of hitherto highly classified photos captured by US aerial reconnaissance. For Zorin—exhausted, weakened by heart trouble—the humiliation was almost too much to bear.

The private diplomacy began as soon as the public diplomacy did. Kennedy wanted to demonstrate American resolve, but he was also very concerned that the crisis could escalate out of control. On Sunday, the day before his dramatic speech, he had confided to presidential aide Arthur Schlesinger, "We will have to make a deal at the end." But he felt "we must stand absolutely firm now. Concessions must come at the end of negotiation, not at the beginning." Having stood firm on Monday, it was time to begin to explore the terms of a potential deal on Tuesday, including exploring the possibility of withdrawing American Jupiter missiles from Turkey in exchange for the

Figure 4.3 US Ambassador Adlai Stevenson presents photographic evidence of Soviet missiles to the UN Security Council (AP/Wide World Photos)

withdrawal of Soviet missiles from Cuba. The president began to pursue possible solutions both through the well-established private channels he had used for the previous two years and through some new, rather unorthodox channels.

Someone close to the White House, possibly Robert Kennedy, asked an American journalist, Frank Holeman, to talk to Bolshakov. Holeman was the one who had originally introduced Bolshakov to Bobby, and he had two things to relate on October 24. The first was that the president was resolute: the missiles had to be withdrawn, and he was prepared to take further steps, if necessary. But, second, Kennedy might be willing to discuss a deal involving Turkish missiles. Perhaps to ensure that Holeman's message was taken seriously, the White House asked another journalist and close Kennedy family friend, Charles Bartlett, to talk to Bolshakov as well. Inexplicably—but possibly because of the confusion surrounding the lack of information—the GRU in Washington failed to report these approaches to Moscow until the following day.

DID KENNEDY ORDER THE JUPITER MISSILES REMOVED BEFORE OCTOBER 1962?

The Eisenhower administration decided in 1957 to deploy Jupiter missiles in Italy and Turkey and Thor missiles in Britain under the auspices of NATO. The purpose was to extend the US nuclear umbrella to important NATO allies in the face of growing Soviet military capability.

One of the persistent myths about the Cuban missile crisis is that Kennedy had ordered American Jupiter missiles withdrawn from Turkey prior to the crisis and was angry to discover that they were still there. The story appeared in Elie Abel's 1966 book *The Missile Crisis* as well as in R. F. K.'s *Thirteen Days*. It was repeated in the 1971 edition of Graham Allison's widely read book *Essence of Decision*.

In fact, there was no such order. Kennedy knew very well the Jupiters were still in Turkey. The Kennedy administration had discussed canceling the deployment—virtually everyone agreed they were unreliable and obsolete and that they contributed little or nothing to Western deterrence since they were such easy targets—but the Turks wanted them as symbols of the American commitment to Turkish defense as well as for their prestige value. For political reasons, the deployment went ahead.

Strictly speaking, Kennedy did not have the authority to remove the Jupiter missiles themselves. These had become Turkish property. He did, however, have authority to remove their warheads, which were under US jurisdiction.

The Jupiter bases in Turkey had become operational only six months prior to the missile crisis. Unbeknownst to the president and the ExComm, the Pentagon officially turned over the first Jupiter base to Turkish forces on October 22, 1962—ironically, the very day of Kennedy's speech.

Late on Tuesday evening, Bobby met with Dobrynin at the Soviet embassy in Washington. The meeting was not particularly constructive, and no offers were made. The two men spent most of their time debating whether or not the United States had been deceived by earlier Soviet statements. The president's brother reminded Dobrynin that the ambassador himself had told him in early September that the Soviets had not placed in Cuba missiles that could reach the United States and had no intention of doing so. That was what Khrushchev had said publicly, Dobrynin replied, and, he added truthfully, that was also his personal understanding. Bobby reminded Dobrynin that the president had relied upon Khrushchev's assurances when attempting to deflect the growing clamor over Cuba as the summer wore on.

President Kennedy's response to Khrushchev's first note was tough, warning of the catastrophic dangers of a nuclear war and suggesting that the Soviet leader may have underestimated the "will and determination" of the

United States. At the same time, however, the letter also emphasized that the steps the United States had taken were moderate and suggested negotiations to resolve the crisis. Kennedy's second letter called on the Soviet leader to observe the OAS declaration but included a personal plea. "I am concerned," said the president, "that we both show prudence and do nothing to allow events to make the situation more difficult to control than it already is." On Wednesday morning, in another tough letter approved by the Presidium, Khrushchev called the blockade "an act of aggression . . . pushing mankind toward the abyss of a world missile-nuclear war." Khrushchev warned that if the United States continued its "piratical actions," the USSR would have to take measures of its own. He insisted once again that Soviet ships would ignore the blockade. But in fact his outrage had already begun to cool. He put out feelers for a possible emergency summit in a reply to a public letter from British philosopher Bertrand Russell and in an impromptu meeting with an American businessman in Moscow, William Knox.

At the ExComm meeting on Wednesday morning, the atmosphere was tense. Photoreconnaissance showed that the Soviets were continuing work on the launch sites for both the R-12 and R-14 missiles and had stepped up their camouflage efforts. Soviet submarines had been detected escorting ships. Although the US Navy had been preparing for days, the blockade officially went into effect only at 10:00 A.M. eastern time on Wednesday, October 24. Within hours, the president would have to decide whether to enforce it and, if so, how. Kennedy's handling of this delicate question proved deft and effective. He ordered the US Navy to allow the first ship that reached the blockade line, an oil tanker, to continue on its way. He allowed an East German passenger ship to pass as well. As R. F. K. reported in *Thirteen Days*, the president wanted to give Khrushchev more time: "I don't want to put him in a corner from which he cannot escape."

It was in this tense atmosphere that the ExComm received the news that the Soviet ships closest to the blockade line—20 in all—had stopped dead in the water or turned back. Dean Rusk leaned over to McGeorge Bundy and remarked, "We're eyeball to eyeball and I think the other fellow just blinked." Among those that turned back were the four transports carrying the entire deployment of R-14 missiles. But the *Aleksandrovsk* had slipped through. With ominous US aerial activity in the area of its intended destination, the port of Mariel, the Soviets decided to divert it to La Isabela. The warheads were safely in Cuba—but stuck aboard ship. La Isabela was not equipped for unloading and storing nuclear weapons.

The US Navy did not in fact board and search a ship until Friday morning, October 26: the *Marucla*, a chartered Lebanese freighter. The ExComm chose it carefully and precisely because it seemed unlikely to be carrying prohibited material. Once inspected, it was allowed to continue. Soviet submarines got rougher treatment. In an effort to show the Soviets that American forces were in control, the US Navy tracked and identified every Soviet sub in the area, dropping practice depth charges and pinging the subs with sonar to force them to surface. One sub was unintentionally damaged in this game of cat and mouse and had to be towed back to the Soviet Union.

Most accounts of the Cuban missile crisis pay little or no attention to the role of the UN, but the UN was indeed a center of great activity. On Wednesday—the day after the first Security Council meeting—acting Secretary-General U Thant sent Kennedy and Khrushchev the first specific proposal to end the crisis. Thant noted with understatement that "the rest of the world is an interested party" in the Soviet–American confrontation and asked both superpowers to refrain from actions that might worsen the situation. He then proposed a stand-down arrangement for a period of weeks in which the Soviets would suspend arms shipments to Cuba and the Americans would suspend the quarantine. He noted that it would "contribute greatly" if construction of military facilities in Cuba were suspended as well. Khrushchev quickly and happily accepted Thant's stand-down proposal but did not explicitly agree to order work halted on the missile sites. Kennedy made clear that he would suspend the quarantine only if the Soviets first stopped work on the missile sites and stopped arms shipments to Cuba. He did, however, agree to begin preliminary talks in New York under UN auspices. These began almost immediately and continued parallel to the discussions carried on in Washington.

Though his stand-down proposal did not fly, Thant did provide Khrushchev with a face-saving way of avoiding a confrontation at sea. The acting secretary-general asked both sides to do their best to avoid one, and on Friday, October 26, Khrushchev indicated that it was in response to this request, rather than the "illegal" blockade, that he had ordered his ships not to challenge the quarantine line.

In Washington for a meeting with the ExComm on Friday, Ambassador Stevenson had little progress to report from New York. In part, he felt, this was because the White House had given him little to offer the Soviets. He thus tried to secure approval in Washington for a deal he thought the Soviets in New York might accept. He predicted they would eventually ask for both a pledge not to invade Cuba and the removal of the Jupiter missiles from Turkey in return for withdrawing their missiles from Cuba. The ExComm overwhelmingly opposed offering up the missiles in Turkey at this point and dismissed Stevenson's request. But Kennedy had already been thinking along these lines and would discuss the issue with his advisers at length the following day.

While the man in charge of American diplomacy, Dean Rusk, was among those opposed to trading the missiles in Turkey, he worked to keep the UN channels open. During its Friday meetings, the ExComm discussed extending the embargo beyond offensive weapons to include POL and ordered nighttime low-level reconnaissance missions. Rusk asked that both options not be pursued immediately on the grounds they would complicate the ongoing talks with Thant and the Soviets in New York.

KHRUSHCHEV AND KENNEDY WAVER

Late Wednesday night, two American reporters were overheard at the National Press Club discussing arrangements to go to Cuba along with American invasion forces. In the wee hours of Thursday morning, the information was passed to a "journalist" who was actually a KGB officer at the Soviet embassy in Washington. At about the same time, Soviet intelligence monitored a highly unusual message: the US SAC was being ordered to go to DEFCON 2 for the first time in its history.

Even before these two new pieces of information reached the Kremlin, Khrushchev had begun to rethink his position. Sending the missiles and other weaponry to Cuba had clearly not protected the Castro regime. If anything, Cuba was now in greater danger of invasion. Khrushchev proposed to his Presidium colleagues that the Soviet Union might offer to dismantle the missile sites in return for a pledge from the United States not to invade Cuba. This would not secure everything Anadyr had been designed to accomplish, Khrushchev conceded; but it might at least secure Cuba, and that would be no minor feat. His colleagues tentatively agreed, but Khrushchev chose to wait a bit before signaling his willingness to deal. He proposed that the entire Presidium go off to Moscow's Bolshoi Theater in a show of calm.

When the news of the SAC alert and the gossip overheard at the National Press Club reached Khrushchev the next morning—Friday, October 26—he decided he could no longer wait. He began dictating a long and rambling letter to Kennedy, offering, in effect, to withdraw:

> I have received your letter of October 25. From your letter, I got the feeling that you have some understanding of the situation which has developed and a sense of responsibility. I value this. . . .
>
> I think you will understand me correctly if you are really concerned about the welfare of the world. Everyone needs peace: both capitalists, if they have not lost their reason, and, still more, Communists, people who know how to value not only their own lives but, more than anything, the lives of the peoples. We, Communists, are against all wars between states in general and have been defending the cause of peace since we came into the world. . . . [I]f indeed war should break out, then it would not be in our power to contain or stop it, for such is the logic of war. I have participated in two wars and know that war ends when it has rolled through cities and villages, everywhere sowing death and destruction. . . .
>
> Let us therefore show statesmanlike wisdom. I propose: we, for our part, will declare that our ships, bound for Cuba, are not carrying any armaments. You would declare that the United States will not invade Cuba with its forces and will not support any sort of forces which might intend to carry out an invasion of Cuba. Then the necessity for the presence of our military specialists in Cuba would disappear. . . .

[W]e and you ought not now to pull on the ends of the rope in which you have tied the knot of war, because the more the two of us pull, the tighter that knot will be tied. And a moment may come when that knot will be tied so tight that even he who tied it will not have the strength to untie it, and then it will be necessary to cut that knot. And what that would mean is not for me to explain to you, because you yourself understand perfectly of what terrible forces our countries dispose. . . .

Entirely by coincidence and unauthorized by Khrushchev, the KGB station chief in the Soviet embassy in Washington decided to try some freelance diplomacy. Aleksandr Feklisov, who operated under the alias of Alexander Fomin, called a well-connected ABC News correspondent he knew, John Scali, and insisted they meet immediately. At the Occidental Restaurant, Feklisov asked Scali if the administration would be interested in an agreement whereby the Soviet missiles would be withdrawn in return for an end to the blockade and an American promise not to invade Cuba. When Scali replied he did not know, Feklisov begged him to find out. Scali immediately reported to the State Department, which passed the information to the ExComm. At 7:30 that evening, Feklisov and Scali met again. This time Scali reported that he was authorized "by the highest authority" to indicate US interest in Feklisov's proposal.

Khrushchev's letter, delayed in transmission, arrived in Washington that evening. The ExComm read it as a confirmation of Feklisov's feeler. Indications seemed to be that the Kremlin was looking for a way out—a welcome sign, from the president's perspective—for intelligence reports clearly showed that work on the missile sites in Cuba was proceeding at a breakneck pace. The Soviets were busily assembling Il-28s. The blockade was having no effect on the weapons systems already present in Cuba, and the ExComm was starting to polarize over the question of what to do next. A majority now wanted to follow up soon with military action of some kind: McNamara favored a limited air strike, Dillon favored a bigger one, McCone and the chiefs wanted to invade. Kennedy was now swimming against the tide. "We will get the Soviet strategic missiles out of Cuba only by invading Cuba or by trading," he said on Friday morning—and in his own mind it was becoming clearer which one he preferred.

THE CRISIS HEATS UP

As Kennedy and Khrushchev were trying to feel their way toward a peaceful resolution, Castro, wittingly or unwittingly, was doing what he could to make a peaceful resolution harder. The consensus of opinion among the Cuban leadership and among the Soviet military in Cuba was that the United States would attack within a matter of days. U-2s were scouring Cuba regularly from on high, and now American fighter jets equipped with cameras were screaming over Cuba at treetop level as well. The Kremlin, eager to avoid a shooting war at this point, refused to allow Soviet air defense forces to fire on American aircraft and had lobbied Castro aggressively to hold Cuban anti-aircraft fire as well. Only the Soviet soldiers manning the S-75s could shoot down high-altitude U-2s, but the Cubans had antiaircraft artillery capable of hitting low-level reconnaissance planes. Castro chafed at the bit. Every US flight that went unchallenged returned to the United States with information that would be valuable in the seemingly inevitable American attack. And every flight that went unchallenged was an affront to Cuba's dignity, as well as an embarrassment to Castro's rule.

On October 26, Castro's patience ran out. He announced that Cuban anti-aircraft forces would start firing on low-level reconnaissance planes the next morning. "We cannot tolerate these . . . overflights," he told Pliyev, "because any day at dawn they're going to destroy all these units." Pliyev sent an urgent coded message to his superiors in Moscow, informing them that the Cubans considered an attack imminent; that he had decided to disperse *techniki* (i.e., to move warheads out of their storage sites and closer to the missiles); and,

Figure 4.4 Warhead storage bunker for R-12 missiles (Courtesy John F. Kennedy Library)

in the event of an American attack, to "employ all available means of air defense." Malinovsky and Khrushchev approved Pliyev's decisions, but in so doing, they clearly were not intending to authorize antiaircraft fire *before* an American attack had begun.

Despite the dire warnings Khrushchev was receiving, not only from Pliyev but from various other sources, on the morning of Saturday, October 27, he was feeling more confident all of a sudden. It had been five days since Kennedy's quarantine speech, and the Americans had not attacked. More and more signals were coming in that the Americans might actually be willing to concede more than just a noninvasion pledge in return for the withdrawal of Soviet missiles. He had seen Bolshakov's report on the Holeman and Bartlett feelers pointing to the possibility that Kennedy might be willing to include the Jupiters in some sort of deal. Moreover, the highly respected American commentator Walter Lippmann had proposed in a newspaper column on October 25 a "face-saving" trade of Jupiters in Turkey for Soviet missiles in Cuba. It was not clear that Lippmann was speaking for the administration, but the Soviets later learned that the columnist had in fact consulted before-hand with a senior American official. The Lippmann formula seemed to Khrushchev to be another sign of American flexibility. "If we could achieve additionally the liquidation of the bases in Turkey," he told his Kremlin col-leagues, "we would win."

Khrushchev now drafted and sent a significantly different letter to Kennedy. This time, Khrushchev emphasized how "irreconcilable" it was for the United States to deploy offensive missiles in Turkey, which "adjoins us," while protesting the placement of Soviet missiles in Cuba. Khrushchev pro-posed the Americans remove their missiles from Turkey and promise not to invade or intervene in Cuba, in return for which he would withdraw the Soviet missiles from Cuba and promise to respect the sovereignty of Turkey. He proposed that both superpowers make the appropriate commitments in the Security Council and reach a formal agreement under the auspices of the UN. Such an accord could "serve as a good beginning" and facilitate agreement on banning nuclear weapons tests—an issue on which, he said, the two coun-tries' positions were "very close together." A test ban, Khrushchev added, would "present humanity with a fine gift."

Aware that the usual diplomatic channels had delayed the previous day's letter, the Kremlin decided to have this one broadcast publicly on Radio Moscow. Simultaneously with the letter to President Kennedy, he had Malinovsky send another message to Pliyev: "You are forbidden," it read, "to apply nuclear warheads to FKR, Luna, Il-28s without authorization from Moscow." The Kremlin evidently wanted no possibly horrific mistakes.

Khrushchev's new letter arrived during Saturday morning's ExComm meeting, as the group was still discussing the less demanding Friday letter. The new one caused a stir. Why all of a sudden had the goalposts moved? What explained the difference in tone? Why had it been broadcast, rather than delivered through the usual channels? Had Khrushchev been overruled by hard-liners? There were other disturbing developments on Saturday as well. Low-level reconnaissance planes were now encountering antiaircraft fire, and some had had to abort their missions; a Soviet ship, the *Grozny*, was approaching the quarantine line, despite Khrushchev's assurances that he would respect it; an American U-2 on a routine air sampling mission in the Arctic that ought to have been canceled as a matter of course had strayed accidentally over Soviet territory, and Soviet fighters were scrambling to intercept it (news that prompted Kennedy to grumble, "There's always some son-of-a-bitch who doesn't get the word"). Most disturbingly of all, a U-2 on a mission over Cuba was overdue. Fears that it had been lost were soon confirmed; it had been shot down by one of the advanced S-75 antiaircraft missiles the Soviets had brought with them to Cuba. The pilot, Major Rudolf Anderson, was dead. The ExComm had agreed previously that if an American aircraft were shot down over Cuba, the United States would respond with an air attack on one or more of the S-75 missile sites. Now, faced with carrying through on this decision, the president hesitated, fearing the consequences if the crisis were to escalate out of control.

The issue that dominated the ExComm's deliberations on Saturday was what to do about Khrushchev's Turkish missile demand. The group as a whole strongly opposed a trade. The government of Turkey emphatically rejected the idea, and many of Kennedy's advisers feared such a deal would split the NATO alliance. After much debate, the group decided to handle the dilemma in a novel way: the president would respond to the first letter, accepting Khrushchev's offer, and publicly ignore the second. This gambit later became known as the "Trollope ploy." There would be no public mention of a trade involving the Turkish missiles. Accordingly, Kennedy wrote to Khrushchev as follows:

> I have read your letter of October 26th with great care and welcomed the statement of your desire to seek a prompt solution to the problem. The first thing that needs to be done, however, is for work to cease on offensive missile bases in Cuba and for all weapons systems in Cuba capable of offensive use to be rendered inoperable, under effective United Nations arrangements.
>
> Assuming this is done promptly, I have given my representatives in New York instructions that will permit them to work out this weekend—in cooperation with the Acting Secretary General and your representative—an arrangement for a permanent solution to the Cuban problem along the lines suggested in your letter of October 26th. As I read your letter, the key elements of your proposals—which seem generally acceptable as I understand them—are as follows:
>
> > 1) You would agree to remove these weapons systems from Cuba under appropriate United Nations observation and supervision; and undertake, with suitable safeguards, to halt the further introduction of such weapons systems into Cuba.

WHO SHOT DOWN THE U-2 AND WHY?

Kennedy and Khrushchev were both puzzled and concerned about the shooting down of Major Anderson's U-2. Khrushchev had given standing orders not to fire on the high-altitude reconnaissance planes, for fear of courting escalation. Kennedy did not know about Soviet standing orders and wondered whether it was a mistake, the result of insubordination, a sign of conflict between Cuban and Soviet forces, or a deliberate escalation. None of these possibilities was cheerful to contemplate.

The real story is complex. The commander of the S-75 battery near Banes, in eastern Cuba, Colonel Georgy Voronkov, received word that an American U-2 had been spotted on radar. Aware that he was forbidden to fire without authorization, he called headquarters for instructions. Pliyev was not in, and his deputy, Lieutenant General Stepan N. Gretchko, told him to wait while he tried to find the commander. As the clock ticked, the U-2 began to move out of range.

Unable to reach Pliyev and concerned that the U-2's photos would be used in an imminent American attack, Gretchko decided that authorizing the shoot-down was the lesser of two evils. He gave the word, and at 10:22 A.M., Voronkov fired three missiles, bringing down Anderson's plane.

Was Gretchko being insubordinate? Or was he merely exercising command initiative, interpreting standing orders liberally? Very clearly, his understanding was the latter. The Cubans were already firing on American aircraft, and the Soviet command in Cuba expected an American attack at any moment. Moscow had given instructions not to fire on U-2s but had also authorized the use of SAMs for self-defense. Gretchko felt the two sets of instructions were in tension.

While Pliyev filed a report on the incident, no officers in Cuba were reprimanded. Malinovsky simply gave Pliyev a mild verbal rebuke that the action had been "too hasty." One reason there may have been no formal sanction is that Khrushchev found the shoot-down useful in his postcrisis diplomacy with Castro: he was able to point to it as a (rare) example of Soviet firmness during the crisis.

The Cubans were forever grateful to the Soviets who downed the U-2 and decorated Voronkov as a war hero.

---

2) We, on our part, would agree—upon the establishment of adequate arrangements through the United Nations to ensure the carrying out and continuation of these commitments—(a) to remove promptly the quarantine measures now in effect and (b) to give assurances against an invasion of Cuba. . . .

But Kennedy was pessimistic that a noninvasion pledge would be enough, and he was inclined to deal away the Jupiters if necessary. "We can't very well invade Cuba, with all this toil and blood it's going to be, when we could

WHO PROPOSED THE "TROLLOPE PLOY"?

Faced on October 27 with two different messages from Nikita Khrushchev containing different proposals, the ExComm advised President Kennedy to respond to the first, which proposed easier terms, and to ignore the second, tougher proposal. This maneuver is now commonly referred to as the "Trollope ploy." President Kennedy publicly accepted Khrushchev's offer to withdraw Soviet missiles from Cuba if the United States would end the blockade and promised not to invade Cuba. He did not publicly respond to Khrushchev's later demand that the United States also withdraw its Jupiter missiles from Turkey. However, unbeknownst to most members of the ExComm, he did give Khrushchev private, informal assurances that the Jupiter missiles would soon be gone.

Bundy coined the term "Trollope ploy," explaining later that he was inspired by Victorian novelist Anthony Trollope, one of whose characters, as he recalled, deliberately interpreted an ambiguous message as an offer of marriage. The reference to Trollope is not precise but roughly corresponds to a scene in Trollope's novel *The American Senator*.

In his memoir, Robert Kennedy claimed credit for the Trollope ploy. The White House tapes indicate, however, that Bundy, Thompson, and Sorensen were thinking along these lines before R. F. K. began pushing the idea, which Sorensen then referred to as "Bobby's formula." Sorensen, we now know, had an active role in editing *Thirteen Days*—so, ironically, he wound up crediting R. F. K. with an idea that was, in part, his own!

have gotten them out by making a deal on the same missiles in Turkey," he mused in the ExComm meeting that afternoon. "If that's part of the record, then I don't see how we'll have a very good war."

When the meeting broke up, the president and a few key advisors—McNamara, Sorensen, Rusk, and Bundy—met to set up a missile trade option. They agreed that Bobby would meet with Dobrynin to deliver a copy of Kennedy's letter, and they authorized him to exercise his discretion as to whether or not to sweeten the deal by agreeing orally to trade away the Jupiters. The president arranged an additional backup plan as well. He asked Rusk to contact his old friend Andrew Cordier, a former UN colleague of U Thant's, asking him to be ready, upon further signal, to give Thant a text that he could represent as his own, proposing a mutual withdrawal of missiles that Kennedy could then accept. Having the proposal come from a respected third party would be much more palatable for Kennedy politically than to be seen giving in to a Soviet demand.

Figure 4.5 The president confers with his brother on the White House veranda (Courtesy John F. Kennedy Library)

Ultimately, the Cordier maneuver proved unnecessary and was never activated. But it was significant because it demonstrated that Kennedy was no longer relying on the ExComm as a decision-making body and was determined to negotiate an end to the crisis. He was taking matters into his own hands.

THE DOBRYNIN MEETING

The president's brother met secretly with Dobrynin at the Justice Department that evening, around 8 P.M. He told the ambassador that the fact that work was continuing on the missile sites was a great concern, and he warned that the downing of the American U-2 could lead to further incidents and a serious escalation of the conflict. The president was under great pressure, Bobby said. While claiming he was not issuing an ultimatum, he said that the Soviet Union had to commit to withdrawing its missiles by the following day, or military action might be unavoidable. Dobrynin asked what offer the United States was making. Bobby gave him a copy of the letter just transmitted to Moscow. Dobrynin then raised the question of a possible withdrawal of American missiles from Turkey.

What followed has been a subject of great controversy ever since. According to the published account in *Thirteen Days*, Robert Kennedy told the ambassador that there could be no deal, no quid pro quo, on such a matter. But he added that the president had wanted those missiles withdrawn for some time and expressed the view that they would be removed after the crisis was resolved.

While speculation arose in the immediate aftermath of the crisis that the president had agreed to remove the missiles from Turkey, Kennedy administration officials consistently insisted that there had been no deal. But in 1989, Theodore Sorensen made an extraordinary confession. As unacknowledged editor of Bobby's memoir, Sorensen said, he had personally changed the original account. Bobby had been very explicit, Sorensen admitted: removal of the missiles from Turkey had been very much part of the deal. Sorensen's admission corroborates the account of the meeting Dobrynin gave Moscow that very night.

What actually happened in Robert Kennedy's office that evening is now clear. Bobby indicated that his brother was willing to include the Jupiters in the agreement to end the crisis. They would be withdrawn, not immediately, but within four to five months. But this part of the deal, Bobby emphasized, had to be kept secret. The United States would never acknowledge it publicly. Only a handful of the president's advisers even knew about it. The NATO allies were told explicitly that there had been no secret agreement. Rusk and McNamara both testified before congressional committees in 1963 that no deal had been struck. Rusk took the same position in the 1980s. As McGeorge Bundy acknowledged in 1988, "We denied in every forum that there was any deal . . . we misled our colleagues, our countrymen, our successors, and our allies."

Even the American participants in the crisis who knew that a missile trade was on the table were generally pessimistic about a peaceful outcome at this point. Robert Kennedy later claimed that his expectation, after his meeting with Dobrynin, was war by Tuesday. McNamara, recalling that Saturday evening sunset over the Potomac as one of the most beautiful he had ever seen, wondered whether he would live to see another. The ball was now firmly in Khrushchev's court. And that, to Kennedy's advisers, was hardly a reassuring prospect.

CLIMAX AND RESOLUTION

Castro was worried. Communications with Moscow had slowed to a trickle. Rumors of deals were in the air. Was Khrushchev getting wobbly? Would he stand up for Cuba? For himself?

> We in Cuba had taken all the steps that were humanly possible [Castro later recalled]. We had talked with the Soviet General Staff, we

explained our views. There were other things I said that may come up sometime later. And when we finished all that, I asked myself, "What is still to be done? What remains to be done? What can I do? What is the last thing I can do?" And I dared to write a letter to Nikita, a letter aimed at encouraging him. That was my intention. . . .

I was afraid that there'd be mistakes, hesitations, because I was already seeing that mistakes were being made, and there were signs of hesitation. I proposed some ideas as to what should be done in the event, not of an air strike, but of an invasion of Cuba in an attempt to occupy it. . . .

What Castro said, in a letter he dictated to Alekseev in the small hours of the morning on October 27, was rather oblique. But Khrushchev interpreted it as a call for a preemptive nuclear strike against the United States. It had precisely the opposite effect of the one Castro intended, for Khrushchev was already beginning to fear that events were getting out of hand and was preparing to throw in the towel.

On the morning of October 28, he awoke not only to Castro's letter but also to the news that an American U-2 had been shot down over Cuba. Pliyev had orders to hold his fire; what had happened? Had his own forces acted against standing orders? Had the Cubans seized an S-75 site? How would Washington react? Would the hard-liners now have the ammunition they needed to push for an attack? Meanwhile, Cuban forces were firing at every American plane they could see. Another might be shot down at any time. What then? Someone in the Soviet military had heard a rumor that the president was preparing another national broadcast for Sunday evening. Would Kennedy announce that military operations against Cuba had begun?

Khrushchev had had enough. He called a formal meeting of the Presidium for noon.

With events moving rapidly, the first item of business was to issue instructions to Pliyev in the event of an American attack. The Presidium decided to allow Soviet forces in Cuba to defend themselves, but Pliyev's instructions made no reference to the use of nuclear weapons. As the Presidium turned to Kennedy's most recent letter, a call came from the foreign ministry informing the Soviet leadership of the report from Dobrynin about his evening meeting with Robert Kennedy. The report not only emphasized that Kennedy was facing mounting pressure to take further military action but also made clear he was offering a secret deal on the Jupiters.

Khrushchev seized the moment. He dictated a response to Kennedy without leaving the meeting. The message promised to dismantle "the arms which you describe as offensive" and to crate and return them to the Soviet Union, in accordance with the terms offered in the president's letter of October 27. To avoid any further delay, he ordered the message to be read immediately over Radio Moscow. News of the announcement sped around the world. Even before the Radio Moscow broadcast, Defense Minister

Malinovsky ordered Pliyev to begin dismantling the recently constructed missile sites.

The news of Khrushchev's announcement interrupted a 9:00 A.M. Sunday meeting at the Pentagon called to plan the American response should the Kremlin reject Kennedy's letter. The joint chiefs, like most other officials, had no knowledge of the secret meetings with Dobrynin or the Jupiter offer. Air Force Chief Curtis LeMay grumbled; he, for one, did not welcome the apparent resolution to the crisis. For days he had been ready and eager to send his planes against Cuba. He wanted to go ahead and attack on Monday anyway. Distrustful of Soviets, LeMay predicted that they would secretly hide some missiles in Cuba. He desperately did not want to let slip this golden opportunity to rid the Western Hemisphere of Castro once and for all.

In the White House, the mood was quite different. There was a sense of profound relief. The president's national security advisor summed up the feelings of many: "Everyone knew who were the hawks and who were the doves," McGeorge Bundy said. "Today was the doves' day." The White House issued a short release that praised Khrushchev's "statesmanlike decision." But the president warned his officials against any gloating about a US victory.

Dobrynin called on Bobby again on Monday. He confirmed officially that Moscow had agreed to withdraw the missiles from Cuba, and he conveyed Khrushchev's personal best wishes to the president and his brother. He also handed over a letter from Khrushchev setting out the terms of the agreement, including the secret deal on the Jupiter missiles. The president's brother returned the letter to the ambassador the next day, refusing to acknowledge it, forcefully adding that there could be no written record of the missile trade. But he gave his word that the Jupiters would soon be gone.

In Havana, Castro was furious. He had had no warning of Khrushchev's decision, which he saw as a capitulation. He felt slighted by the lack of consultation. He had been surprised enough to learn on Saturday that Khrushchev had all of a sudden proposed to pull the missiles out of Cuba if Kennedy pulled his missiles out of Turkey, as though Cuban security were some bargaining chip he could cheaply trade away. Hearing on the radio that Khrushchev proposed pulling out the missiles in return for a worthless American pledge not to invade was almost unbelievable.

Khrushchev wrote to Castro urging restraint and trying to justify his actions. Breathing no word to his Cuban ally of the secret missile trade, he insisted that Castro had been right that an American attack was imminent and that there had been no time to consult. Khrushchev tried to make the case that securing Kennedy's pledge not to attack Cuba was a major victory, securing Cuba's future. But Castro was having none of it:

> Countless eyes of Cuban and Soviet men who were willing to die with supreme dignity shed tears upon learning about the surprising, sudden and practically unconditional decision to withdraw the weapons.

... We knew, and do not presume that we ignored it, that we would have been annihilated, as you insinuate in your letter, in the event of nuclear war. However, that didn't prompt us to ask you to withdraw the missiles, that didn't prompt us to ask you to yield. . . .

There are not just a few Cubans, as has been reported to you, but in fact many Cubans who are experiencing at this moment unspeakable bitterness and sadness.

The imperialists are talking once again of invading our country, which is proof of how ephemeral and untrustworthy their promises are. Our people, however, maintain their indestructible will to resist the aggressors and perhaps more than ever need to trust in themselves and in that will to struggle.

We will struggle against adverse circumstances, we will overcome the current difficulties and we will come out ahead, and nothing can destroy the ties of friendship and the eternal gratitude we feel toward the USSR.

Castro would not, in other words, break with Moscow over Khrushchev's mistreatment. But as the following weeks would prove, he could threaten to derail the agreement. And this is precisely what he proceeded to do.

CHAPTER 5

Aftermath

IT'S NEVER OVER till it's over. And, despite the collective sigh of relief the world felt on October 28, the Cuban missile crisis was not over. Exactly what had been agreed to between Washington and Moscow on that tumultuous weekend quickly became a matter of dispute. Cuba refused to cooperate and thwarted the inspections called for in the Kennedy–Khrushchev agreement. An unresolved issue emerged. The United States made additional demands. And the Kennedy administration backed away from one of its key promises. Together, these developments extended the Cuban missile crisis well beyond the original, now fabled, thirteen days.

REMOVING THE MISSILES FROM CUBA

Within hours of Nikita Khrushchev's acceptance of the deal on October 28, Soviet soldiers were dismantling the missile sites. Their eventual destruction was thorough. The MRBMs were not exactly "crated," as Khrushchev's statement had promised, but were removed with dispatch and taken to Cuban ports. No large-hatch ships were on hand since many of those used in earlier shipments were carrying the R-14 missiles and had been stopped by the blockade. The Soviets therefore loaded the 42 R-12 missiles onto the decks of available ships. They even gave the United States an inventory of the missiles and a shipping schedule. On November 8, the Pentagon announced that all known MRBM and IRBM missile sites in Cuba had been dismantled; the next day, the last Soviet ship carrying R-12s and related equipment left Cuba. Three days later, Khrushchev officially confirmed that all the missiles had been removed.

Rumors began circulating in Washington almost immediately that the Soviets were hiding nuclear weapons in Cuban caves, a mark of the pervasive distrust of Soviets in general, and of Khrushchev in particular. The only way to be sure that the Soviets had withdrawn what they said they would withdraw was to conduct on-site inspections—a daunting task, given the size

Figure 5.1 R-12 missile site under demolition (Courtesy John F. Kennedy Library)

of Cuba, even if Castro were to permit it. But he would not. Feeling humiliated, ignored, and utterly distrustful of Kennedy's noninvasion pledge, Castro demanded on October 29 that the United States cease violating Cuban airspace (i.e., suspend all surveillance flights), lift not merely the blockade but also the long-standing economic embargo against Cuba, terminate subversive activities, prevent what Castro called the "piratical attacks" of others, and close down the naval base at Guantánamo. These "Five Points," as this set of demands became known, went well beyond the matters immediately under dispute between the superpowers; they encompassed, from the Cuban government's perspective, most of the outstanding issues of US–Cuban relations. As such, they were the real issues, Castro felt, with which the United States and the Soviet Union should have been dealing. But the United States ignored them. The Soviets did nothing more than pay lip service to them, eager as they were to liquidate the crisis as quickly as possible.

The one ace up Castro's sleeve was the fact that he could thwart international inspections, a key provision of the Kennedy–Khrushchev agreement.

CASILDA PORT
6 NOVEMBER 1962

6 MISSILE TRANSPORTERS

TRUCK

TRUCK CRANE
TRUCK

CANVAS COVERED PROBABLE CRANE

Figure 5.2   Soviet missiles and equipment loaded for return to USSR (note shadow of US RF-101 *Voodoo* reconnaissance plane in foreground) (Courtesy John F. Kennedy Library)

Not only was Castro miffed that Khrushchev had failed to consult him before agreeing to the inspection condition; he felt intensely that, as a matter of sovereignty and principle, Cuba could not submit to such an indignity. In a meeting with U Thant in Havana on October 30, Castro summarily rejected each of the on-site inspection arrangements suggested by the acting secretary-general.

The Americans and Soviets had to find a work-around to verify the withdrawal of the R-12s. The fact that no large-hatch ships were available proved to be fortuitous. Once outside Cuban waters, Soviet soldiers pulled back the tarpaulins covering the missiles on the decks of their ships so that American reconnaissance planes could photograph them (a task several Soviet soldiers would later describe as the most humiliating of their professional careers). The United States was therefore able to observe that the same number of missiles the Soviets claimed to have sent to Cuba had also been withdrawn. The White House expressed satisfaction with this informal verification; but,

Figure 5.3 US Navy patrol aircraft monitoring Soviet missile withdrawal (Courtesy John F. Kennedy Library)

not surprisingly, skeptics in the United States did not. Rumors persisted for decades that the Soviets had left some number of missiles behind.

Khrushchev worried about Castro's belligerent intransigence. There was a danger not only that he would delay or derail a final settlement but also that he would provoke something serious. The quarantine was still in place; American forces remained on high alert; preparations for military action continued.

There was a danger, too, of a permanent rupture in Soviet–Cuban relations. To calm Castro down and to secure his cooperation as far as possible, Khrushchev dispatched to Havana his most trusted fixer, Anastas Mikoyan.

Mikoyan's mission was long and difficult and began badly. En route to Havana, he stopped in New York, where Adlai Stevenson handed him a list of the weapons systems the United States considered "offensive" and demanded to have withdrawn. The list was much longer than Mikoyan expected. To appease Cuba, Mikoyan had to make a statement in New York endorsing Castro's Five Points, though he knew they were unworkable and would only complicate matters. And then, almost as soon as he arrived in Cuba and just a couple of hours into his first meeting with Castro, an aide handed him a telegram from Moscow informing him that his wife had died. Though the news was a terrible personal blow, it had a salutary effect on his mission: Castro could see his pain, and it softened him. "Theirs was a long-standing marriage," Castro later recalled. "They were very close. We saw

WHAT WAS THE STATUS OF THE NONINVASION PLEDGE?

Kennedy's noninvasion pledge had been specifically conditional upon inspections. Aware of this, Khrushchev attempted repeatedly to secure a formal American commitment not to invade Cuba. He was not successful. Washington was increasingly reluctant to make such a formal commitment. Both the State Department and the Pentagon were opposed. Congress took no action to endorse it. In fact, American officials began stating publicly that Cuba's refusal to allow on-site inspection of the missile sites had rendered the noninvasion commitment null and void.

On January 7, 1963, after a few more weeks of talking, American and Soviet negotiators in New York, like two exhausted boxers, simply called it quits. Ambassador Stevenson and Vasily Kuznetsov wrote a joint letter to the UN acting secretary-general indicating that they had not been able to resolve all the issues before them. This meant that the United States never formally communicated its noninvasion commitment to the UN. Nevertheless, Stevenson and Kuznetsov said they had reached a satisfactory degree of understanding, which at least allowed the Security Council to take the crisis off its agenda.

In 1970, Secretary of State Henry Kissinger became the first American official to affirm that the Kennedy administration's commitment not to invade Cuba was "still in force." As Dean Rusk had noted during the crisis itself, of course, both the Rio Treaty and the UN charter already prohibited an American invasion of Cuba; but this fact did not receive much public attention in the United States.

Mikoyan cry. But he decided to stay here in Cuba and continue with the talks rather than go back to the USSR" for his wife's funeral. Castro called it a "very generous gesture."

THE CUBAN BOMBER CRISIS

When Khrushchev told Kennedy he would remove the weapons that "you call offensive," he meant only the R-12 missiles and the strategic nuclear warheads (the R-14s had never arrived). The Kennedy administration, however, understood anything that was technically capable of reaching the United States from Cuba to be an "offensive" weapon. So the list Stevenson handed Mikoyan included the following:

1. Surface to surface missiles (R-12s, R-14s, FKRs, Sopkas) and Il-28 bombers

2. Bombs, air to surface rockets, and guided missiles

3. Warheads for any of the above weapons

4. Mechanical or electronic equipment to support or operate the above items, such as communications, supply, and missile-launching equipment, including Komar-class motor torpedo boats.

Of these, the Il-28s would ultimately prove the most difficult on which to agree. On October 28, in the wake of an apparent agreement to end the crisis, President Kennedy was less than fully adamant about demanding the withdrawal of these bombers. He did not want to get "hung up" on them. But the Il-28's combat range meant that it could reach targets in Florida, and it was known to be nuclear-capable. Kennedy ultimately felt those were reasons enough to insist that the bombers be withdrawn; had he known that Khrushchev had provided six of them with nuclear bombs, he would certainly have gotten hung up on them.

Khrushchev replied to the American demands on November 4, with exasperation. "It is hard for us to understand," he wrote, "what aim is being pursued by the introduction of that list." It only aggravated matters. In Cuba, Mikoyan assured the Castro government that Moscow would never agree to this "new" American demand. Kennedy tried to reassure Khrushchev, saying that the only item on the list he cared about, other than the MRBMs and IRBMs, was the Il-28 force. As the bombers were becoming the focus of domestic attention in the United States, Kennedy felt he had to insist upon their withdrawal. Arguably, the Kremlin should not have been surprised by the inclusion of the Il-28s. Kennedy had mentioned in his October 22 speech that "jet bombers capable of carrying nuclear weapons are now being uncrated and assembled in Cuba while the necessary air bases are being prepared." Interestingly, the Kennedy administration contemplated insisting as well on the withdrawal of Soviet MiG-21s from Cuba but in the end did not, even though these aircraft could carry nuclear weapons, were faster, and had a longer range than the older Il-28s.

Days passed. In Havana, Mikoyan sheepishly had to tell Castro that Moscow now wanted to remove the Il-28s as well. This fresh irritant only worsened Castro's mood. Most of the Il-28s were originally intended for the Cuban air force and armed only with conventional weapons. Castro could not understand how Kennedy could possibly construe these planes as offensive. In an attempt to grease the skids, Bobby Kennedy met Bolshakov again on November 9, offering him a choice of options. One was that the Soviets would commit to removing the bombers "as soon as possible." The other was to promise that only Soviet personnel would fly the disputed aircraft. Bobby telephoned Bolshakov only an hour later to withdraw the latter offer: the bombers had to go. But Khrushchev seized the opportunity to try a Trollope ploy of his own, agreeing on November 11 that only Soviet crews would pilot the Il-28s. Probably suspecting this would not be enough, he also offered a "gentleman's word" that the bombers would be removed when "the conditions are ripe," by which he meant when Castro agreed. Khrushchev hinted that Castro was giving him trouble, and he asked Kennedy for more time. Kennedy countered by saying that if Moscow accepted a thirty-day timeline for the withdrawal of the Il-28s, he would immediately lift the quarantine. In so doing, he was implicitly lifting the inspection condition as well.

At this point, Khrushchev heard from Mikoyan, still in Cuba, that the ever-independent Castro had once again ordered his antiaircraft forces to fire on American reconnaissance planes. Khrushchev was furious and even toyed briefly with the idea of threatening to pull all Soviet personnel out of Cuba. He decided he could wait for the Cubans no longer. He would withdraw the Il-28s unilaterally. When the Americans insisted they needed a reply prior to the president's press conference scheduled for November 20, Khrushchev agreed to the thirty-day timeline.

That evening, announcing that the Soviets had agreed to withdraw the bombers, Kennedy terminated the quarantine. To some extent, this was pro forma, as the US Navy had been under orders not to stop and inspect Soviet ships for weeks. To reassure the skeptics, he insisted that overhead reconnaissance would continue, but he quietly canceled the low-level flights (U-2 flights continued at a pace of roughly one per day). The Pentagon reduced the alert status of American forces and prepared to release reservists. The Cuban missile crisis was finally winding down.

Figure 5.4 Soviet Ilyushin Il-28 (NATO designation "Beagle") jet light bomber (Reproduced with permission from Jane's Information Group)

There was one last loose end, though the Kennedy administration never caught wind of it. The Kremlin's original intention was to leave tactical nuclear weapons in Cuba. On October 30, Malinovsky ordered the strategic nuclear weapons returned to the USSR, but Pliyev began training Cuban forces in the use of the Lunas, FKRs, and Il-28s almost immediately thereafter. When Castro heard Kennedy's speech on November 20 assuring the American people that all the nuclear weapons had left Cuba, he called in Mikoyan to ask whether the tactical nuclear weapons had been withdrawn as well. He wondered because Khrushchev had promised never to agree to withdraw the Il-28s and had done exactly that. For all Castro knew, Khrushchev might agree to pull out absolutely everything, leaving Cuba completely exposed. It was vital, Castro felt, that Cuba retain at least the tactical nuclear weapons.

Castro's behavior during the month of November gave Soviet leaders pause. His unwillingness to cooperate in the settlement of the crisis and his irresponsible decision to resume shooting at American planes demonstrated once again his impetuousness and moodiness. They began to doubt the wisdom of leaving tactical nuclear weapons in Cuba. A diplomatic indiscretion was the final straw. "[W]e still have tactical nuclear weapons, which must be kept," Foreign Minister Raúl Roa cabled Cuba's UN ambassador, Carlos Lechuga, on November 20. The Americans did not even know there were tactical nuclear weapons in Cuba, and if they were listening in on Cuban conversations, the entire settlement might suddenly unravel.

Thus, when Castro called in Mikoyan on November 22 to inquire about the tactical weapons, Mikoyan decided—apparently on his own authority, lacking clear instructions at this point from Moscow—that he would inform Castro that the tactical nuclear weapons would also be withdrawn. They could not be turned over to Cuba, he stated, because Soviet law prohibited transferring nuclear weapons of any kind to any other country. Nor were they being withdrawn under American pressure since the United States did not even know they were there. Moscow simply felt that this was the wise course. Cuba would continue to enjoy the protection of the Soviet nuclear deterrent but only from a distance and not from Cuban soil. Castro was unhappy but decided not to make a further issue of it. Putting on a game face, he saw Mikoyan off at the airport on November 26, expressing satisfaction with his visit. In December, the last nuclear warhead left Cuba for the Soviet Union.

As for the Jupiter missiles in Turkey, Kennedy kept his word. On Saturday, October 27—around the time his brother was meeting with Dobrynin—President Kennedy asked a Pentagon official to prepare plans for withdrawing the Jupiter missiles. On October 29, McNamara initiated a confidential process to remove the Jupiters from both Turkey and Italy. The head of the task force appointed to effect the withdrawal told those assembled for its first meeting "the missiles are going to be out of there by April 1 if we have to shoot them out."

WHAT BECAME OF THE SOVIET NUCLEAR WEAPONS WITHDRAWN FROM CUBA?

Precise records are not available, but the R-12 and R-14 missiles were most likely returned to their original sites in the USSR and retargeted on Western Europe. The USSR eventually ceased production of both systems in the mid-1960s, after building and deploying a total of approximately 500 R-12s and 100 R-14s. The existing missiles, however, remained part of the Soviet nuclear arsenal for more than two decades.

During the 1980s, these same weapons became embroiled in yet another nuclear controversy: the fractious "Euromissile" debate. The Soviet Union had developed and deployed a sophisticated new mobile missile, the RSD-10 (NATO designation SS-20 "Saber"), capable of hitting targets in Western Europe. In response, the United States deployed Pershing II missiles in Europe capable of hitting targets in the Soviet Union. The escalation of the nuclear arms race these systems represented was a source of considerable tension.

In 1987, the Intermediate-range Nuclear Forces (INF) Treaty led to the elimination of these systems, as well as the remaining R-12s and R-14s. The treaty, signed by US President Ronald Reagan and Soviet leader Mikhail Gorbachev, signaled the beginning of the end of the Cold War.

As far as is known, the tactical nuclear weapons withdrawn from Cuba were returned to the Soviet inventory. A few Il-28s remained on active duty with the Soviet military until the 1980s, though most were retired in the 1960s.

Visitors to Cuba today can see a collection of several of the Soviet missiles at the center of the crisis—minus their warheads and engines—quietly occupying a corner of a park not far from El Morro Castle east of Havana harbor. The unmarked weapons sit discreetly behind the Fortaleza de San Carlos de la Cabaña; even seasoned Cuban tour guides often do not know of their existence. The photograph of the R-12 missile shown in Figure 2.1 (p. 35) is part of this collection.

The United States raised the Jupiter issue at the semiannual NATO ministerial meeting in December 1962, arguing that they were obsolete and unnecessary and ought to be withdrawn. The deterrent function they had served could be more easily and more effectively provided, the Americans insisted, by a Polaris submarine kept on station in the eastern Mediterranean. The Italians, while irritated, did not offer much resistance. Turkey was more reluctant, but after the Italians had agreed and after the British announced that U.K.-based Thor missiles would be phased out, the Turkish government ultimately agreed as well.

The Jupiter missiles were so obsolete they not worth salvaging. They were literally scrapped. Their nuclear warheads were returned to the United States by late April 1963—almost, but not quite, within the four to five months Robert

Kennedy had promised in his October 27 conversation with Dobrynin. The Soviets never demanded verification of their removal, but McNamara did. He insisted on being shown pictures of the dismantled Jupiters.

THE DOMESTIC AND INTERNATIONAL PUBLIC REACTION

John F. Kennedy's performance during the Cuban missile crisis earned him both widespread praise and points in the polls. His approval rating among Americans jumped to well over 70 percent. His party performed better in the November 1962 congressional elections than expected.

Despite public denials, rumors nevertheless persisted that the White House had made a secret deal with the Soviets involving the Jupiters in Turkey. They were in part laid to rest by a timely article that was portrayed as a semi-authoritative inside account of the workings of the White House during the Cuban missile crisis. Kennedy's friend, reporter Charles Bartlett, approached him to ask whether he and a coauthor, Stewart Alsop, might write an article. Kennedy was more than happy to cooperate, on condition that he could see it prior to publication. One of McGeorge Bundy's aides told Bartlett that Adlai Stevenson had proposed a Jupiter trade but that the president had flatly rejected the idea. It is not clear why Bartlett was so gullible on this point, given that he himself had met with Georgi Bolshakov during the crisis, almost certainly at the request of the White House, to float a trial balloon about just such a deal. At any rate, Kennedy did not correct this false version of events when he saw the draft. After the article appeared in the *Saturday Evening Post*, Kennedy asked his aide Arthur Schlesinger to assure Stevenson that he, Kennedy, had not spoken to Bartlett or Alsop. That, of course, was untrue. Stevenson was being "hung out to dry" to help deflect speculation about the secret deal.

The public reaction to the Cuban missile crisis among America's allies was at least as positive as the domestic American response. Most Latin Americans and their governments rallied to the United States' side. In Canada, John F. Kennedy was more popular than Prime Minister Diefenbaker, and the Canadian public was highly critical of its own government's apparent foot-dragging during the crisis. In January 1963, the United States Information Agency (USIA) conducted public opinion surveys in major allied countries in Europe that showed that Europeans had a very favorable image of the United States after the crisis, had more confidence in its ability to deal with world problems, and believed it was trying to avoid war. At the same time, Europeans had a very negative image of the Soviet Union, as they had for most of the early Cold War period.

At the same time, the USIA survey suggested the crisis raised questions in some minds about the simple "black and white" Cold War pattern. The survey respondents were also asked if the missile crisis had changed their views of the United States and the Soviet Union. While most said it had not, some believed it had. Of the latter group, those whose views of the United States had changed, most now saw America more positively. They tended to appreciate that the United States had stood up to the USSR and defended Western interests. At the same time, most of those who said the crisis had changed their view of the USSR (a minority, to be sure) also tended to see the USSR in a more positive rather than more negative way. They were more positive not because the Soviets had placed missiles in Cuba but because Khrushchev's decision to withdraw the missiles showed more flexibility and reasonableness than might have been expected. When then asked directly why the crisis was resolved peacefully, more survey respondents in both the United Kingdom and Germany actually pointed to "Soviet moderation" than American military strength. The survey also showed most believed the United States ought to withdraw its missiles from Turkey, a step the Kennedy administration, of course, had agreed to and was in fact already taking.

In these ways, the Cuban missile crisis marked for some Europeans the beginning of the end of stereotypical Cold War images. It thus laid the seeds of what later became a strongly pro-détente psychology in Europe. That attitude was an important element behind the Euromissile debate in the 1980s and the negative European reaction to the hard-line anti-Soviet rhetoric of the early Reagan administration.

STEPS TOWARD DÉTENTE: THE HOT LINE AND TEST BAN

The difficulties and delays the Kremlin and the White House experienced communicating with each other during the crisis left a powerful impression on many of the participants. The hours lost in translating, encoding, transmitting, decoding, and delivering urgent messages, many felt, might well have been the difference between peace and war. In response, the United States and the Soviet Union negotiated what became known as the "Hot Line" agreement in the first months of 1963. Intended to provide for rapid communication in time of emergency, it created, initially, a direct teletype connection between the two capitals via a physical line running through London, Copenhagen, and Helsinki. The Hot Line has been maintained ever since, although, on one occasion, a Finnish farmer, carelessly ploughing his field, managed to sever it.

Contrary to popular belief, the Hot Line has never been a telephone link. Many felt that the disadvantages of voice communication in crisis outweighed the advantages. Useful communication is sometimes hindered by the requirement to respond immediately and by translation on-the-fly. But the technology has been updated several times and now permits facsimile as well as text transmission. Originally, the American terminal was placed in the Pentagon, but it was later moved to the White House. Today, multiple redundant links, including satellite links, provide for secure communication between Russian and American leaders even when they are not in Moscow or Washington. It is not known how many times the Hot Line has been used, although it is generally acknowledged that the first time was during the Six Day War in 1967. Arguably, its symbolic value has been even greater than its practical value.

Talks designed to help rein in the arms race by restricting nuclear tests had been going on for years prior to the missile crisis but had been hopelessly deadlocked. Here again, the issue of on-site inspections proved to be a major stumbling block. While it was technically possible to detect tests conducted in the atmosphere, it was more difficult to detect and monitor underground tests reliably. It was possible, many felt, for a state to hide an underground nuclear testing program; thus, they believed a comprehensive test ban was unverifiable. Concerned that the Soviets might conduct secret tests, the United States sought an agreement calling for a significant number of on-site inspections; the Soviets feared these would be used for espionage purposes and were willing to agree only to a few.

Nikita Khrushchev raised the matter of the nuclear test ban negotiations in a letter to Kennedy on October 30, 1962. "We now have conditions," he wrote, "ripe for . . . signing a treaty on cessation of tests of thermonuclear weapons." Kennedy responded in favorable albeit general terms, but months would pass before the two countries reached an agreement and not without difficulties. The Treaty Banning Nuclear Weapons Tests in the Atmosphere, in Outer Space and Under Water (the Partial Test Ban Treaty [PTBT], sometimes referred to as the Limited Test Ban Treaty [LTBT]) was signed by the United States, the USSR, and the United Kingdom in August 1963. It was a watershed, marking an important new era in arms control; but while it represented a genuine step toward reducing superpower tensions and building mutual confidence, it fell short of the comprehensive test ban that many had advocated, for it prohibited only nuclear tests "or any other nuclear explosion" in the atmosphere, in outer space, or under water.[1] Not until 1996 would the major nuclear powers agree to the terms of a comprehensive test ban, although the US Senate refused to ratify the treaty.

---

1. The LTBT was approved by the US Senate, with limited opposition, and came into force in October of the same year. France, which first successfully tested a nuclear weapon in 1960, did not sign; neither did China, which tested in 1964. Both France and China eventually abandoned atmospheric testing, however, and there have been no nuclear tests in the earth's atmosphere since 1980. The result has been a significant decline in the levels of dangerous airborne radionuclides and considerable human health benefits globally for more than a generation.

Conclusion

ONE OF THE most striking features of our tale is the contrast between the pre-crisis and crisis performances of John F. Kennedy and Nikita Khrushchev. Before the crisis, neither understood just how insecure and threatened the other felt. Each assumed the other saw the world as he did. Each failed to anticipate what the other might do. Each failed to think through the possible consequences of his own actions. The result was that they stumbled blindly into a confrontation that neither expected or desired. But once in it, standing on the brink and staring into the abyss of nuclear war, they both scrambled brilliantly. Once their respective shock and anger had passed (Kennedy's triggered by the discovery of the missiles, Khrushchev's triggered by Kennedy's blockade speech), they began to realize just how badly they had misunderstood each other and made Herculean efforts to keep matters from spinning out of control—in part by trying to cultivate, under the most difficult conditions imaginable, precisely the kind of mutual understanding that they had earlier so badly lacked.

Their errors in the years before the crisis were a function of a kind of blindness. Perhaps willfully, and perhaps not, they simply did not bother to try to understand where their statements and actions might lead. By threatening and harassing Cuba and by attempting to persuade Khrushchev of his toughness, Kennedy succeeded only in provoking precisely the kind of challenge he feared most. Khrushchev's bluster and bluff, his constant threats about Berlin, and his attempts to bully and cow Kennedy succeeded only in making both Cuba and the Soviet Union more vulnerable to American power. Neither Kennedy nor Khrushchev was the first mover in this deadly game, and it is pointless to ask who was responding to whom: it was a dynamic interaction that simply got out of hand.

It was fortunate that Kennedy took almost an entire week to choose his response to the Soviet deployment. If he had had to respond right away, his anger would have gotten the best of him and he would have authorized military action. Air strikes alone would not have been enough to ensure the destruction of Soviet strategic nuclear capability in Cuba, and Kennedy would have faced considerable pressure to follow up with an invasion. Indeed, many in the United States would have pushed for an invasion not merely to rid Cuba of Soviet missiles but to rid Cuba of Castro as well. In early October, the CIA thought there were perhaps 4,000 or 5,000 Soviet troops in Cuba. On October 22, the estimate was between 8,000 and 10,000. In fact, there were close to 42,000 Soviet soldiers on the island, and they were armed with tactical nuclear weapons. It is easy to imagine US Marines, attempting to establish beachheads in Cuba, vaporized by desperate Soviet defenders whose only hope of avoiding defeat was to use the most powerful tools at their disposal. What then? Could Kennedy have resisted the clamor to retaliate? Would the conflict have spread to Turkey or Berlin? Where would it have stopped? Uncertainty played on Kennedy's mind, and when his anger cooled, he became very focused on persuading Khrushchev to withdraw the missiles in a way that minimized the danger of escalation. So keen was Kennedy to avoid a shooting war that he ignored many of his own advisers and put in place a peaceful exit option that he felt Khrushchev might accept.

Khrushchev's anger had time to cool, too. Kennedy announced the quarantine on Monday evening, Washington time; but it did not come into effect until Wednesday morning. Kennedy did not even attempt to enforce it until Friday and even then did so in a symbolic, cautious way. The United States used no violence and took no irrevocable actions that would have put Khrushchev in a position from which he had no choice but to use violence in return. In his correspondence with Khrushchev early in the public phase of the crisis, Kennedy even pressed him, in an almost paternal way, to calm down and sober up. "I am concerned," he wrote on October 23, "that we both show prudence and do nothing to allow events to make the situation more difficult to control than it already is."

Khrushchev did. Like Kennedy, he was careful to take no irrevocable steps down the path to confrontation. At the climax of the crisis, he, like Kennedy, feared that conflict might be imminent and stepped decisively back from the brink.

Both Kennedy and Khrushchev had to deal with hawks. Both were under pressure to hang tough. The US military, convinced that America's strategic nuclear superiority and local conventional superiority in the Caribbean gave them a free hand, felt confident that the Soviets would back down. The Soviet military, confident that their admittedly inferior but still adequate strategic nuclear capability meant that Kennedy would be deterred from attacking, felt confident that they did not have to. It is fortunate indeed that Kennedy and Khrushchev were inclined to be skeptical and had the courage to resist the pressure. As Khrushchev related in his memoirs, when he asked his generals whether they could guarantee that a refusal to withdraw the missiles would not lead to global nuclear war, they looked at him "as though I were out of my mind or, what was worse, a traitor. So I said to myself, 'To hell with these maniacs.' "

The fact that Kennedy and Khrushchev had time to grope their way to a settlement meant also that they had time to learn in greater detail the nature of their predicament. They were not simply struggling against each other; they were not simply struggling against their own hawks; they were also struggling against chance.

Governments and militaries are complex systems, and things go wrong. When large militaries are geared for battle, tightly wound up to spring into action at a moment's notice, things going wrong can have rapid and catastrophic consequences. At the climax of the crisis, Kennedy and Khrushchev both had dramatic lessons in this. The Soviets could easily have believed that the hapless American pilot whose U-2 strayed over Siberia returning from a routine mission—one that should have been canceled—was conducting prestrike reconnaissance. What Kennedy does not seem to have known, as far as we are aware, is that because of the heightened alert, the Alaska Air Command fighters that scrambled from Galena Air Force Base to escort the pilot back into American airspace were carrying live nuclear Falcon antiaircraft missiles. What would have happened if they had encountered the MiGs that scrambled to intercept the U-2?

Meanwhile, another U-2 was shot down over Cuba in violation of standing orders to hold fire. Neither Khrushchev nor Kennedy knew why this had happened, but both, fortunately, suspected that it might be inadvertent.

Thus, at the climax of the crisis Kennedy and Khrushchev began to focus on the dangers of things spinning out of control. What they did not know would only have reinforced their desire to bring things to a rapid conclusion. SAC, for instance, launched a Titan ICBM from Vandenberg Air Force Base on October 26, in accordance with its pre-planned testing schedule. This particular missile was not carrying a nuclear warhead, but other ICBMs at Vandenberg *were*—again, owing to the heightened alert. Fortunately, the Soviets never detected the launch, or they might have misinterpreted it as a first strike. At Malmstrom Air Force Base in Montana, officers at a Minuteman ICBM silo were having difficulty getting their launch system to work. Eager to comply with the order to go to DEFCON 2, they simply jerry-rigged it, bypassing the normal safeguards. They could have fired the nuclear missile under their command any time they wanted. On the morning of October 28, just before Khrushchev broadcast his agreement to withdraw Soviet missiles from Cuba, US radar operators at Moorestown, New Jersey, reported a missile launch from Cuba. A training tape had mistakenly been feeding into the Moorestown monitors. In the Atlantic, the US Navy was relentlessly harassing one of the Soviet Foxtrot-class submarines. With practice depth charges exploding all around, oxygen running low, and the internal temperature soaring to 122 degrees Fahrenheit, the sub commander could not take it any more and ordered his nuclear torpedo armed and readied for firing. "There may be a war raging up there and we are trapped here turning somersaults!" he cried. "We are going to hit them hard. We shall die ourselves, sink them all but not stain the navy's honor!" Fortunately, the submarine's political officer managed to calm him down.

Castro was not attuned to the dangers of inadvertent war. He was convinced that a *deliberate* war was about to break out at any moment. So convinced was he that the United States would use the opportunity to destroy the Cuban Revolution that his main concern was simply to make sure that they paid as dearly as possible for the attempt. He did not have a death wish; he was not behaving irrationally, given what he believed; but what he believed was wrong. Kennedy was not eager for war; he was doing his best to avoid one. Lacking empathy with Kennedy, Castro had no inkling of this.

The Cuban missile crisis therefore stands as a dramatic lesson in the vital importance of empathy. When adversaries fail to understand each other—when they make no effort to put themselves in each other's shoes—they fall victim to mirror-imaging, wishful thinking, and misperception. Rarely are these as dangerous as they were in 1962, fortunately; but in a nuclear world, they are clearly matters of great concern.

Whether or not Castro learned this lesson, Kennedy and Khrushchev did. Doing so enabled them to work out a mutually satisfactory solution to the crisis. It enabled them to begin exploring ways of reducing superpower tension, improving their ability to communicate, and lowering the risks of future crises. The United States and the Soviet Union still had many tangible conflicts of interest, of course; the experience of the Cuban missile crisis did not eliminate them. Rivals they were, and rivals they would remain. But as long as Kennedy and Khrushchev were at the helm, they would be rivals who were highly sensitized to the paramount importance of staying as far away from the brink as possible. Kennedy captured the new sensibility better than anyone in a famous graduation speech at American University on June 10, 1963. "No government or social system is so evil that its people must be considered as lacking in virtue," said the president. "[L]et us not be blind to our differences—but let us also direct attention to our common interests and to the means by which those differences can be resolved. And if we cannot end now our differences, at least we can help make the world safe for diversity. For, in the final analysis, our most basic common link is that we all inhabit this small planet. We all breathe the same air. We all cherish our children's future. And we are all mortal."

Sadly, neither Kennedy nor Khrushchev lingered long enough to leave the kind of imprint on US–Soviet relations, or on world politics more broadly, that they might otherwise have done. When Kennedy was shot and killed in Dallas on November 22, 1963, he was succeeded by Lyndon Johnson, a man who was little more than a bystander during the Cuban missile crisis and who seems not to have absorbed its lessons anywhere near as fully. Johnson did become aware of the dangers of provoking inadvertent war. He did his best during his presidency to try to stabilize superpower relations and to contain regional conflicts, so as not to become embroiled in a similarly dangerous confrontation again. Thus, for example, he acted decisively to prevent conflict over Cyprus from erupting into all-out war between Turkey and Greece in 1964 and to prevent India and Pakistan from coming to blows over Kashmir in 1965. But what he learned from the crisis most of all, it seems, was that a carefully measured application of force can serve American interests. He does not appear to have learned much from the crisis about the drawbacks of military force as an instrument of statecraft. Nor does he appear to have learned much about the importance of cultivating empathy. Thus, when faced with decisions in Vietnam, Johnson took pains to avoid provoking Chinese or Soviet intervention but put misplaced faith in the utility of American military force as a political or diplomatic tool. His faith proved misplaced, in large part, because he had no empathy for his adversary in Vietnam. Like most Americans in official Washington, he thought the enemy was international communism, not Vietnamese nationalism; and he did not understand that the North Vietnamese and the National Liberation Front were willing to bear any burden, and pay any price, to "liberate" and unite their country. Their overwhelming imperative was to drive foreign powers from their soil. The result was an unnecessary war that left the United States profoundly shaken, as well as 58,000 Americans—and some three million Vietnamese—dead.

Khrushchev was ousted in a bloodless coup on October 14, 1964. Among the many charges his colleagues levied against him were recklessness and adventurism in Cuba. His successor, Leonid Brezhnev, was, like Johnson, more of a bystander than active participant in the missile crisis. In many ways the antithesis of Khrushchev, Brezhnev was no gambler; and his eighteen-year rule was characterized by stasis as much as anything else. But not having felt as Khrushchev did the acute urgency of building a more stable basis for superpower relations, he proved unimaginative and not particularly energetic in cultivating opportunities to do so. For the most part, he simply allowed the Cold War to stay cold.

Castro has outlived both Kennedy and Khrushchev by a long margin. Never quite losing the revolutionary's fire in the belly, Castro never quite forgave Moscow for Cuba's mistreatment. Nor did he ever come to trust the United States to accept an independent, socialist Cuba. But while emotional and headstrong, Castro has also always been clever and capable of great pragmatism. He turned the missile crisis to his advantage in his relations with the Soviet Union, essentially milking his Soviet patrons to the tune of billions of dollars' worth of military and economic aid year after year. The hostility of the United States proved to be perhaps his greatest political asset, and he has taken great advantage of that, too. Throughout his reign, Castro has been able to blame the United States and its embargo for Cuba's economic woes. He has been able to justify his own authoritarianism and his intolerance for dissent as necessary expedients, in view of the United States' implacable hostility. Still, as became clear in international conferences on the crisis held

Figure 6.1 Castro visits Khrushchev in Soviet Georgia, May 1963 (Sergei Khrushchev Collection)

in Havana in 1992 and 2002, Castro eventually did come to appreciate how close the world came to nuclear war in 1962 and he did come to see the role that misperception, misjudgment, and lack of empathy played in bringing about such a dangerous situation.

It is fascinating to speculate on what might have happened had Kennedy lived and Khrushchev lasted longer. Many knowledgeable observers are convinced, for example, that Kennedy would have managed to avoid a heavy American commitment in Vietnam, in part because—unlike Johnson—he was skeptical of his advisers in the military and intelligence communities who would have been among those most enthusiastically pushing him to get involved. There is some evidence that Kennedy was even contemplating attempting a rapprochement with Cuba after the 1964 election.

He put out a number of tentative feelers just before he died. Whether there was any chance of success even if he did follow through with a significant effort is open to debate; American hostility may have been too valuable to Castro to give up.

While Brezhnev was less concerned with finding ways of reducing superpower tensions than was Khrushchev in the immediate aftermath of the crisis, he was generally careful about upsetting the apple cart, and during his rule the Soviet Union managed to work out a set of norms, rules, and procedures to help reduce the chance of conflict. This "security regime," as some have called it, limited the numbers and types of weapons the Soviets could send to Cuba and committed all three countries to formal and informal communication and consultation for the purpose of reducing uncertainty. From time to time, "mini-crises" would provide the opportunity for all three to learn exactly what was and was not acceptable behavior. In 1969 and 1970, for example, the Soviets learned that the United States would not tolerate a Soviet naval base in Cuba capable of servicing nuclear submarines. In 1978, they learned that the United States *would* tolerate the export to Cuba of a downgraded version of the MiG-23 "Flogger" jet fighter. Some of the interactions over Cuba were statesmanlike and mature, but others bordered on the absurd. In 1979, for example, the United States "discovered" a Soviet combat brigade in Cuba, prompting strident calls for its withdrawal. But, as many in the US intelligence community had known all along, the brigade had been in Cuba continuously since 1962.[1]

There would never be another confrontation quite like October 1962. Although the United States and the Soviet Union weathered other crises afterward and while relations between the two countries were never warm, they did manage to avoid direct confrontations. They took care not to surprise each other in their respective areas of vital interest. They did fight numerous proxy wars, fueling conflict all over the globe; but they never again came so close to nuclear war, precisely because it was such a frightening experience the first time. In this sense, as Fyodor Burlatsky would later say, the Cuban missile crisis was "a bad thing with a good result."

But the legacy of the Cuban missile crisis has arguably been much less positive than it might have been. History since 1962 is as much the story of lessons forgotten or missed as it is of lessons learned. Among the most

---

1. The incident gave the Soviets another opportunity to embarrass themselves in front of Castro, which they duly proceeded to do by claiming (falsely) that the brigade was merely a "training" center. Castro's fears that the Soviets would never stand up to the United States on Cuba's behalf were only further buttressed the following year when Brezhnev flatly refused a request, following the election as US president of the notoriously anticommunist and anti-Castro Ronald Reagan, to give an explicit security guarantee. "We can't fight in Cuba because you are 11,000 kilometers away from us," the Soviets replied. "Are we going to go all that way just to have our faces smashed?"

significant of these, perhaps, is also one of the oldest: that Great Powers ignore the needs, desires, and perspectives of smaller countries at their peril. American insensitivity to Cuban aspirations in the nineteenth and twentieth centuries laid the groundwork for the Cuban missile crisis. American insensitivity to Vietnamese aspirations led to quagmire in Southeast Asia. The Soviet Union stumbled into its own version of Vietnam in Afghanistan, where from 1979 to 1989 it fruitlessly sought to prop up friendly puppet regimes in the face of determined anticolonial resistance. More than a million Afghans died in the struggle against Soviet occupation, as did 15,000 Soviets. Perhaps the most significant casualty of all was the Soviet Union itself. Battered, bled, and no longer sure of its place and mission in the world, the USSR was unable and unwilling to hold itself together in 1989 in the face of mounting domestic and international pressures for change.

We see this missed lesson in our own time in Iraq. If the experience of Vietnam undermined American confidence in the utility of force, it did so only temporarily. With a move from a conscript to an all-volunteer professional military—and with the experience of a dramatic one-sided victory in the 1991 liberation of Kuwait—the United States became the world's acknowledged preeminent military power in the wake of the Soviet collapse. The US conquest of Iraq and ouster of its brutal dictator Saddam Hussein in March and April 2003 was, from an operational military perspective, child's play. "Mission Accomplished," proclaimed a star-spangled banner on the bridge of the USS *Abraham Lincoln* as President George W. Bush stated on May 1 that "major combat operations in Iraq have ended." But the carnage and chaos had only begun. Almost immediately, a deadly insurgency sprang up that tapped a seemingly limitless wellspring of resentment, much of it directed at and sustained by the American presence itself. With a little empathy and local knowledge—and a great deal less wishful thinking—this might easily have been foreseen.

The Cuban missile crisis may have resulted in large part from a clash of incompatible worldviews and mindsets, but one thing Kennedy, Khrushchev, and Castro all agreed upon in 1962, consciously or not, was that Great Powers care only about other Great Powers. It may be difficult to cultivate empathy with one's adversaries both powerful and weak, but we submit that the primary lesson of Cuba—and Vietnam, Afghanistan, and Iraq—is the paramount importance of trying. This was a lesson Kennedy and Khrushchev learned primarily by staring down what Theodore Sorensen poignantly called "the gun barrel of nuclear war." But just as Kennedy was primed to learn this lesson in part by reading Barbara Tuchman's *The Guns of August*, so might future leaders be primed to learn it by reflecting on the Cuban missile crisis itself.

Bibliographic Essay

READERS WHO WISH to explore various aspects of the Cuban missile crisis in more detail have a wealth of material from which to choose. In this essay, we discuss some of the more notable and more influential works. Toward the end, we also provide some guidance on Web sources and films.

EARLY TREATMENTS OF THE CRISIS

A flurry of books appeared in the years immediately after the crisis, almost all written in a highly dramatic style. They make for excellent reading and often succeed well in communicating the sense of drama surrounding the crisis, but they are unreliable as histories. The authors of these early books had no access to Soviet or Cuban sources and generally parroted the version of events that the Kennedy administration was eager to promote. In this version, a strong and resolute John F. Kennedy stood up to Nikita Khrushchev's brazen opportunistic challenge and forced him to back down. It is perhaps not surprising that this theme dominates much of the early literature since some of the better-selling books in this vein were written by people who were either in the administration or closely connected to it: for example, Arthur M. Schlesinger, Jr., *A Thousand Days: John F. Kennedy in the White House* (New York: Houghton Mifflin, 1965), and Theodore C. Sorensen, *Kennedy* (New York: Harper & Row, 1965).

As we noted in the Introduction, the best-known early account is Robert F. Kennedy, *Thirteen Days: A Memoir of the Cuban Missile Crisis* (New York: Norton, 1969). R. F. K.'s memoir contains relatively few outright falsehoods, but it is a masterwork of spin. The book is based on R. F. K.'s diaries, but it was carefully edited by Ted Sorensen. Very clearly a campaign document, the book is particularly misleading on the subject of the missile trade. Nevertheless, it does an excellent job of conveying the atmosphere in the White House.

Somewhat more probing but still limited by a lack of reliable information are David Detzer, *The Brink: Cuban Missile Crisis, 1962* (New York: Crowell,

1972); Henry M. Pachter, *Collision Course: The Cuban Missile Crisis and Coexistence* (New York: Praeger, 1963); and Elie Abel, *The Missile Crisis* (Philadelphia: Lippincott, 1966). Among political scientists, one of the best-known and most influential books is Graham T. Allison, *Essence of Decision: Explaining the Cuban Missile Crisis* (Boston: Little, Brown, 1971), which used the missile crisis as a vehicle for developing and contrasting three "models" of foreign policy decision making: the rational actor model, the organizational process model, and the bureaucratic politics model. A more recent second edition has attempted to bring the scholarship of the book somewhat up to date but at the cost of further muddying what were already murky conceptual waters: Graham T. Allison and Philip Zelikow, *Essence of Decision: Explaining the Cuban Missile Crisis,* 2d ed. (New York: Longman, 1999).

Of the works with a significant memoir element that deal with the crisis in whole or in part, the best by far is McGeorge Bundy, *Danger and Survival: Choices About the Bomb in the First Fifty Years* (New York: Random House, 1988), both because it has the benefit of some distance and because of its analytical character. Also useful is Roger Hilsman, *To Move a Nation: The Politics of Foreign Policy in the Administration of John F. Kennedy* (New York: Doubleday, 1967), although readers of this book will be forgiven for mistakenly thinking Hilsman was at the center of action. Other interesting accounts, in descending order of insightfulness, include George W. Ball, *The Past Has Another Pattern: Memoirs* (New York: Norton, 1982); Maxwell D. Taylor, *Swords and Plowshares* (New York: Norton, 1972); Abram Chayes, *The Cuban Missile Crisis* (New York: Oxford University Press, 1974); Dean Rusk, *As I Saw It* (New York: Norton, 1990); Robert S. McNamara, *The Essence of Security: Reflections in Office* (New York: Harper & Row, 1968); Paul H. Nitze, *From Hiroshima to Glasnost: At the Center of Decision—a Memoir* (New York: Grove Weidenfeld, 1989); and Pierre Salinger, *With Kennedy* (Garden City, NY: Doubleday, 1966).

Most of the critical reactions to the early literature—much of it by so-called revisionists—appeared in book reviews. Some of the early revisionist work began asking hard questions, for example, about a possible secret missile trade; but the dominant theme was that Kennedy had overreacted, unnecessarily risking nuclear war. A good overview and analysis is James A. Nathan, "The Missile Crisis: His Finest Hour Now," *World Politics*, vol. 27 (1976), pp. 256–281.

THE SECOND WAVE: "CRITICAL ORAL HISTORY"

In the mid-1980s, the process of declassifying old government documents began to shed new light on what had become the standard story of the missile crisis. Not long afterward, Soviet President Mikhail Gorbachev encouraged a policy of *glastnost'*, or "openness," that permitted Soviets to participate in reexaminations of the crisis for the first time. Cubans began to participate shortly thereafter. The main impetus for this second wave of missile crisis scholarship was a project conceived and organized by James G. Blight, using a method he came to call "critical oral history." A rare example of methodological innovation in historical scholarship, critical oral history brings together declassified documents, scholars, and former decision makers for intensive, multiday discussions, with often surprising results. Blight and his colleagues have applied the method to other events as well (most notably, the Vietnam War), but the missile crisis project was the first and longest, comprised of six major conferences over a thirteen-year period. See James G. Blight and David A. Welch, *On the Brink: Americans and Soviets Reexamine the Cuban Missile Crisis*, 1st ed. (New York: Hill & Wang, 1989), and 2d ed. (New York: Noonday, 1990); Bruce J. Allyn, James G. Blight, and David A. Welch, eds., *Back to the Brink: Proceedings of the Moscow Conference on the Cuban Missile Crisis, January 27–28, 1989* (Lanham, MD: University Press of America, 1992); James G. Blight, Bruce J. Allyn, and David A. Welch, *Cuba on the Brink: Castro, the Missile Crisis, and the Soviet Collapse*, 1st ed. (New York: Pantheon, 1993), and rev. and enl. ed. (Lanham, MD: Rowman & Littlefield, 2002). A good short overview of some of the early results of this project is Raymond L. Garthoff, *Reflections on the Cuban Missile Crisis*, rev. ed. (Washington, D.C.: Brookings, 1989), while a fascinating analysis of the implications for decision making is James G. Blight, *The Shattered Crystal Ball: Fear and Learning in the Cuban Missile Crisis* (Savage, MD: Rowman & Littlefield, 1990).

RECENT ACCOUNTS

The collapse of the Soviet Union in 1990 led to a rapid opening of Soviet archives, greatly enriching the documentary record available to scholars. This has permitted a wave of retellings and reexaminations that draw upon and integrate a broader range of material. The best-detailed history is Aleksandr Fursenko and Timothy Naftali, *"One Hell of a Gamble": Khrushchev, Castro and Kennedy, 1958–1964* (New York: Norton, 1997), which is highly readable as well as very informative. A breakthrough work on the Soviet side of the crisis, with heavy emphasis on the military aspects, is Gen. Anatoli I. Gribkov and William Y. Smith, *Operation Anadyr: US and Soviet Generals Recount the Cuban Missile Crisis* (Chicago: Edition Q, 1994). A useful recent mid-length treatment that stresses the military dimensions of the crisis is Norman Polmar and John D. Gresham's *DEFCON-2: Standing on the Brink of Nuclear War During the Cuban Missile Crisis* (Hoboken, N.J.: Wiley, 2005).

Now that the documentary and testimonial record is so rich, it is possible to look closely into particular aspects of the crisis that received very little attention in the decades immediately following. A prime example is Philip Nash, *The Other Missiles of October: Eisenhower, Kennedy, and the Jupiters, 1957–1963* (Chapel Hill: University of North Carolina Press, 1997), which is the first comprehensive study of the Jupiter missile story. Students of intelligence assessment have always been fascinated by the crisis, but early works were severely hampered by a lack of reliable information—e.g., Arnold L. Horelick, "The Cuban Missile Crisis: An Analysis of Soviet Calculations and Behavior," *World Politics*, vol. 16, no. 3 (April 1964), pp. 363–389, and Roberta Wohlstetter, "Cuba and Pearl Harbor: Hindsight and Foresight," *Foreign Affairs*, vol. 43, no. 4 (July 1965), pp. 691–707. Readers interested in the subject now have access to a reasonably comprehensive treatment that includes, for the first time, a detailed discussion of Cuban intelligence: James G. Blight and David A. Welch, eds., *Intelligence and the Cuban Missile Crisis* (London: Frank Cass, 1998). For a very thorough memoir by a US intelligence analyst, see Dino A. Brugioni, *Eyeball to Eyeball: The Inside Story of the Cuban Missile Crisis*, ed. Robert F. McCort (New York: Random House, 1991).

Not all of the new material is reliable. Jerrold L. Schecter and Peter S. Deriabin, *The Spy Who Saved the World: How a Soviet Colonel Changed the Course of the Cold War* (New York: Charles Scribner's Sons, 1992), for example, is overly sensational and exaggerates the role of Soviet spy Oleg Penkovsky in the affair (Penkovsky did provide Western intelligence agencies with some useful information but hardly "saved the world"). Some of the best new material is buried in books that have other fish to fry. A good example of this is Scott D. Sagan, *The Limits of Safety: Organizations, Accidents, and Nuclear Weapons* (Princeton, NJ: Princeton University Press, 1993), which documents in detail many of the most frightening mishaps during the crisis in the course of conducting a broader exploration of organizational challenges to crisis management.

BACKGROUND AND HISTORY

There is a great deal of material available on the events and personalities of the years, decades, and even centuries preceding the missile crisis. Solid treatments of US foreign policy toward Latin America in general, or Cuba in particular, include Dexter Perkins, *A History of the Monroe Doctrine* (Boston: Little, Brown, 1955); Julius W. Pratt, *America's Colonial Experiment: How the United States Gained, Governed, and in Part Gave Away a Colonial Empire* (New York: Prentice Hall, 1950); Donald Marquand Dozer, *Are We Good Neighbors? Three Decades of Inter-American Relations, 1930–1960* (Gainesville: University of Florida Press, 1959); Ernest R. May, *Imperial Democracy: The Emergence of America as a Great Power* (New York: Harcourt, Brace & World, 1961); and Basil Rauch, *American Interest in Cuba, 1848–1855* (New York: Columbia University Press, 1948). For an unapologetically benign view of US foreign policy toward the region, see Samuel Flagg Bemis, *The Latin American Policy of the United States: An Historical Interpretation* (New York: Harcourt, Brace and Company, 1943). Two of the most influential works covering the background of US–Soviet relations are Adam B. Ulam, *Expansion and Coexistence: Soviet Foreign Policy, 1917–73*, 2d ed. (New York: Praeger, 1974), and William Taubman, *Stalin's American Policy: From Entente to Detente to Cold War* (New York: Norton, 1982).

Among the best works on Castro and the Cuban Revolution are Tad Szulc, *Fidel: A Critical Portrait* (New York: Morrow, 1986); Maurice Halperin, *The Rise and Decline of Fidel Castro* (Berkeley: University of California Press, 1972); K. S. Karol, *Guerrillas in Power: The Course of the Cuban Revolution*, trans. Arnold Pomerans (New York: Hill & Wang, 1970); Hugh Thomas, *The Cuban Revolution* (New York: Harper & Row, 1977); and Andrés Suárez, *Cuba, Castroism and Communism, 1959–66* (Cambridge, MA: MIT Press, 1967). Carlos Franqui, *Family Portrait with Fidel*, trans. Alfred MacAdam (New York: Vintage, 1985), is engaging but not entirely reliable. A number of excellent books have been written on the Bay of Pigs, among which the most valuable narrative histories are Peter Wyden, *Bay of Pigs: The Untold Story* (New York: Simon & Schuster, 1979), and Trumbull Higgins, *The Perfect Failure: Kennedy, Eisenhower and the CIA at the Bay of Pigs* (New York: Norton, 1987). Thomas G. Paterson's "Fixation with Cuba: The Bay of Pigs, Missile Crisis and Covert War Against Castro," in his edited volume *Kennedy's Quest for Victory: American Foreign Policy, 1961–1963* (New York: Oxford University Press, 1989), is provocative. For a recent critical oral history exploration, see James G. Blight and Peter Kornbluh, eds., *Politics of Illusion: The Bay of Pigs Invasion Reexamined* (Boulder, CO: Lynne Rienner, 1997). Particularly useful on the cloak-and-dagger story are Thomas Powers, *The Man Who Kept the Secrets: Richard Helms & the CIA*, 1st ed. (New York: Knopf, 1979); Jon Elliston, *Psywar on Cuba: The Declassified History of US Anti-Castro Propaganda* (Melbourne: Ocean Press, 1999); and Jonathan Nashel, *Edward Lansdale's Cold War* (Amherst: University of Massachusetts Press, 2005). The last of these focuses more on the quixotic figure of Lansdale and his adventures in Vietnam than it does on Cuba or Operation Mongoose but is nonetheless an engaging read.

There are now a number of fascinating studies of Soviet foreign policy in the period leading up to the crisis, of which the trailblazer is undoubtedly Vladislav Zubok and Constantine Pleshakov, *Inside the Kremlin's Cold War: From Stalin to Khrushchev* (Cambridge, MA: Harvard University Press, 1996). There are several fascinating biographies of Khrushchev, but the standout is William Taubman, *Khrushchev: The Man and His Era* (New York: Norton, 2003). Worth exploring also, however, are Khrushchev's own memoirs—Nikita S. Khrushchev, *Khrushchev Remembers*, ed. Strobe Talbott (Boston: Little, Brown, 1970); Nikita S. Khrushchev, *Khrushchev Remembers: The Glasnost Tapes*, trans. Jerrold L. Schecter and Vyacheslav V. Luchkov (Boston: Little, Brown, 1990)—and those of his son—Sergei Khrushchev, *Khrushchev on Khrushchev: An Inside Account of the Man and His Era*, trans. William Taubman (Boston: Little Brown, 1990), and Sergei Khrushchev, *Nikita Khrushchev and the Creation of a Superpower* (University Park: Pennsylvania State University Press, 2000), the latter of which is less memoir than scholarly analysis.

AFTERMATH

The literature on US–Cuban, US–Soviet, and Cuban–Soviet relations since the missile crisis is generally excellent. Particularly valuable, in our view, are Wayne S. Smith, *The Closest of Enemies: A Personal and Diplomatic Account of the Castro Years* (New York: Norton, 1987), written by a former head of the US Interests Section in Havana, and James G. Blight and Philip Brenner, *Sad and Luminous Days: Cuba's Struggle with the Superpowers After the Missile Crisis* (Lanham, MD: Rowman & Littlefield, 2002). Raymond L. Garthoff's *Détente and Confrontation: American–Soviet Relations from Nixon to Reagan*, rev. ed. (Washington, D.C.: Brookings, 1994), is a monumental work that repays careful study. Well worth reading also are Nicola Miller, *Soviet Relations with Latin America 1959–1987* (Cambridge: Cambridge University Press, 1989), and Wayne S. Smith, ed., *The Russians Aren't Coming: New Soviet Policy in Latin America* (Boulder, CO: Lynne Rienner, 1992).

DOCUMENT COLLECTIONS AND WEBSITES

The release of previously classified documents has resulted in a deluge of new information that would be well nigh impossible to wade through and exploit were it not for the efforts of a number of scholars (and institutions) to cull them and organize them. Early valuable efforts include Mary S. McAuliffe, ed., *CIA Documents on the Cuban Missile Crisis* (Washington, D.C.: Central Intelligence Agency History Staff, 1992); *The Secret Cuban Missile Crisis Documents* (Washington, D.C.: Brassey's, 1994); and Laurence Chang and Peter Kornbluh, eds., *The Cuban Missile Crisis, 1962: A National Security Archive Documents Reader*, rev. ed. (New York: New Press, 1998). Voyeurs will be unable to resist Ernest R. May and Philip Zelikow, *The Kennedy Tapes: Inside the White House During the Cuban Missile Crisis* (Cambridge, MA: Harvard University Press, 1997), which is perhaps best used in conjunction with Sheldon Stern's *The Week the World Stood Still: Inside the Secret Cuban Missile Crisis* (Stanford, CA: Stanford University Press, 2005). Those interested in an orientation to some of the issues surrounding documentation should read Raymond Garthoff, "Documenting the Cuban Missile Crisis," *Diplomatic History*, vol. 24, no. 4 (Spring 2000), pp. 297–303.

A great deal of valuable material is now available on the Web. Perhaps the richest trove is that heroically gathered by the true masters of the Freedom of Information Act request, the National Security Archive at George

Washington University in Washington, D.C. (http://www.gwu.edu/~nsarchiv). The site of record for previously secret material from the Eastern bloc is the Cold War International History Project (CWIHP) at the Woodrow Wilson Center for Scholars (http://wwics.si.edu/index.cfm?fuseaction=topics.home&topic_id=1409), which publishes a series of working papers as well as the indispensable *CWIHP Bulletin* (http://wwics.si.edu/index.cfm?topic_id=1409&fuseaction=topics.publications). Also valuable are the US Department of State's *Foreign Relations of the United States* volumes, many of which—including the complete Kennedy administration collection—are available online as well (http://www.state.gov/www/about_state/history/frus.html). The Miller Center of Public Affairs at the University of Virginia maintains an excellent site on the White House tapes (http://www.whitehousetapes.org/), where visitors can find both audio clips and transcripts. Finally, there are a number of general sites devoted to the missile crisis on the Web, of which some of the most useful for those without much background are the *Fourteen Days in October* site (http://library.thinkquest.org/11046/), the John F. Kennedy Library and Museum's *The World on the Brink* site (http://www.jfklibrary.org/cmc_intro.html), and the CNN *Cold War* episode 10 site (http://www.cnn.com/SPECIALS/cold.war/episodes/10/).

FILM

Finally, it is worth saying a few words about cinematic treatments of the crisis. These are not, strictly speaking, "sources" for further study; but they are nevertheless engaging and thought-provoking. As a rule of thumb, they ought not to be treated as historically accurate; but film is sometimes capable of communicating a sense of the look and feel of the crisis that books, articles, and Websites simply cannot.[1]

The best known, of course, is the *Thirteen Days* we discuss in the Introduction. As historical drama, *Thirteen Days* is a better film than one might have expected but worse than one might have hoped. Hollywood rarely makes an effort to be accurate, but the filmmakers in this case did, enlisting scholars of the crisis as consultants and drawing liberally upon fairly recent material. They invented very little, and while they reordered certain things, conflated others, and left a great deal out, the story they tell is certainly a recognizable one.

Of the crucial plot elements, two inaccuracies stand out. The first is the portrayal of Kenneth O'Donnell, who was not a central figure in the crisis.

---

1. The book that does the best job is Alice L. George, *Awaiting Armageddon: How Americans Faced the Cuban Missile Crisis* (Chapel Hill: University of North Carolina Press, 2003).

Cynics have noted that O'Donnell's son helped underwrite the film and that this may account for the embellished role. But Kevin Costner had to play someone, and he neither looks nor sounds like any of the principals. (He neither looks nor sounds like O'Donnell, for that matter; but viewers are unlikely to know this.) The second inaccuracy is that the film overplays civil–military tensions. The president and the chiefs disagreed on many things, of course; but their interactions were all civil. There were only two truly heated exchanges: one between McNamara and Admiral George Anderson over quarantine procedures, which the film divides into two separate scenes (one between J. F. K. and Anderson at the White House and one between McNamara and Anderson at the Pentagon), and one between the president and Air Force Chief General Curtis LeMay after the announcement of the October 28 deal, where LeMay argued for invading Cuba notwithstanding the settlement.[2]

What the film does best is convey Kennedy's emotional evolution after the discovery of the missiles: from shock to anger to belligerence to doubt to fear and finally to caution. Bruce Greenwood, playing Kennedy, badly overacts; the real President Kennedy usually managed to maintain an appearance of calm.

Sadly, the film makes no effort to contextualize the crisis or to explore the Soviet and Cuban angles. Most treatments of the crisis are badly unbalanced as it is, so it is a shame that the film only reinforces the tendency to obsess about the American experience. But there is a sense in which art imitates life in this respect since decision makers in Washington knew little of the Soviets and Cubans at the time either. And with but two hours to work with, it is hard to know how much of the Soviet and Cuban perspectives the filmmakers could reasonably have attempted to cover.

Thirteen Days is not the only dramatization of the crisis. The 1974 made-for-television movie *The Missiles of October* is entertaining as well, though it is not a glitzy production, not being especially high-budget. Based loosely on R. F. K.'s memoir, the film is highly inaccurate, but the performances of William Devane as J. F. K. and Howard Da Silva as Khrushchev are both memorable. For sheer entertainment value, perhaps the best film ever made that had anything to do with the crisis is Alfred Hitchcock's 1969 adaptation of the Leon Uris novel *Topaz*, a Cold War spy thriller that uses the missile crisis as a backdrop for what is an entirely fictional tale. For insight into what it was like to live through the crisis in postrevolutionary Cuba, nothing is more powerful or more effective than Tomás Gutiérrez Alea's 1968 dramatization

---

2. Among the things entirely invented was O'Donnell's attempt to hush up information about Cubans firing on US reconnaissance planes and LeMay's attempt to extract information about this from one of the pilots O'Donnell had sworn to secrecy. There was no attempt to hide this information from the chiefs. There were also a number of inconsequential mistakes, such as anachronistic ships and planes and rain in Washington on October 27.

of Edmundo Desnoes's novel *Memorias del subdesarrollo* (*Memories of Under-development*), often considered one of the finest Cuban films ever made.

Several documentaries have been made on the crisis, and these make a more serious effort at factual accuracy than do the dramatizations. One of the best is difficult to find but worth the effort if the effort is successful: ABC News' *The Missiles of October: What the World Didn't Know* (1992), narrated by Peter Jennings. While it contains a few factual inaccuracies, it also contains an unrivaled treasure trove of contemporaneous footage from US, Soviet, and Cuban sources and is superior to documentaries produced by NBC, NHK, and the BBC, though the latter—*Cuba: The Other Side of Armageddon* (2002)—efficiently counters the early Camelot court history version of events. Easier to find than any of these dedicated documentaries is Errol Morris's Oscar-winning *The Fog of War: Eleven Lessons from the Life of Robert S. McNamara* (2003), only part of which deals with the Cuban missile crisis and only in a partial way; but it is a brilliant work that affords unprecedented insight into one of the chief players in the drama. The film is best studied in conjunction with the companion volume by James G. Blight and janet M. Lang, *The Fog of War: Lessons from the Life of Robert S. McNamara* (Lanham, MD: Rowman & Littlefield, 2005).

Index